Ortho's Houseplant Encyclopedia

Created and designed by
the editorial staff of
ORTHO BOOKS

Project Editor
Marianne Lipanovich

Writers
Larry Hodgson
Dr. Charles C. Powell

Additional Writing by
Donald M. Vining

Ortho Books

Publisher
Richard E. Pile, Jr.

Editorial Director
Christine Jordan

Production Director
Ernie S. Tasaki

Managing Editors
Robert J. Beckstrom
Michael D. Smith
Sally W. Smith

System Manager
Linda M. Bouchard

Editorial Assistants
Joni Christiansen
Sally J. French

Marketing Specialist
Daniel Stage

Distribution Specialist
Barbara F. Steadham

Sales Manager
Thomas J. Leahy

Technical Consultant
J. A. Crozier, Jr., Ph.D.

Address all inquiries to:
Ortho Books
Chevron Chemical Company
Consumer Products Division
Box 5047
San Ramon, CA 94583

Chevron Chemical Company
6001 Bollinger Canyon Road
San Ramon, CA 94583

Acknowledgments

Photo Editor
Pamela K. Peirce

Editorial Coordinator
Cass Dempsey

Copyeditor
David Sweet

Proofreader
Edwin Lin

Indexer
Trisha Feuerstein

Composition by
Laurie A. Steele

Associate Editor
Sara Shopkow

Production by
Studio 165

Separations by
Color Tech Corp.

Lithographed in the USA by
Webcrafters, Inc.

Designers
Names of designers are followed by the page numbers on which their work appears.
Carlos Sanchez, Sanchez-Ruschmeyer Interior Design, San Francisco, Calif.: 7
Ruth Soforenko Associates, Palo Alto, Calif.: 1, 9, 10
John Wheatman, John Wheatman & Associates Inc., San Francisco, Calif.: 4–5, 7, 8

Special Thanks to
Adachi Florists and Nursery, El Cerrito, Calif.;
American Plant Life Society, San Diego, Calif.;
American Rose Society, Shreveport, LA; Pamela Bain;
Gary Beck; Judith Becker; Benefit Guild of the East
Bay, Piedmont, Calif.; Nathan Bennett; Berkeley
Horticultural Nursery, Berkeley, Calif.; Jane Birge;
Cactus Gems, Cupertino, Calif.; Conservatory of
Flowers, Golden Gate Park, San Francisco, Calif.; Mr.
and Mrs. Jonathan W. B. Cosby; East Bay Nursery,
Berkeley, Calif.; Jon Dixon; William D. Ewing;
Floorcraft, San Francisco, Calif.; Geoffrey A. Gatz;
Dorothy Gawienowski; JIL Design Group Inc.,
Carmichael, Calif.; Alan Krosnick; Kenneth and
Marilyn Lavezzo; Eli Lew; Living Green, Plantscape
Design, San Francisco, Calif.; Magic Gardens, Berkeley,
Calif.; Marie's Adoptable Violets, Healdsburg, Calif.;
Ornamental Horticulture Department of City College of
San Francisco; Plants Unlimited Inc., San Lorenzo,
Calif.; Rainbow Garden Nursery and Bookshop, Vista,
Calif.; Red Desert Cactus, San Francisco, Calif.;
Shelldance, Pacifica, Calif.; Sloat Nursery (Wawona St.
Store), San Francisco, Calif.; Strybing Arboretum
Society, San Francisco, Calif.; Phyllis Sutton, San
Francisco Decorator's Showroom; Tommy's Plants, San
Francisco, Calif.; Tralelia Twitty; Bruce Alan Van
Natta; Charlotte Vrooman; Barbara Waldman, Designer
Preview, San Francisco, Calif.; Jacqueline Young

Photographic Plant Stylist
JoAnn Masaoka Van Atta

Photographers
Names of photographers are followed by the page numbers on which their work appears. R = right, C = center, L = left, T = top, B = bottom.
All photographs are by Michael McKinley except for the following:
William H. Allen: 58B
Josephine Coatsworth: 24T
Richard W. Lighty: 36B
John A. Lynch: 101B
Robert E. Lyons: 89B
Tovah Martin: 26T, 43TL, 45B, 56C, 61C, 92B, 93T, 101C, 104B
Joe Mazrimas: 74T
Jack Napton: 20C, 27T, 47B, 59T, 71T
Ortho Photo Library: 22T, 49TL, 49CB
Pam Peirce: front cover top center, front cover center left, front cover center right, front cover bottom center, 17C, 19B, 21T, 21C, 21B, 24B, 25T, 31T, 32T, 33B, 34B, 35TL, 35TR, 35BL, 35BR, 37B, 38B, 39T, 42B, 43B, 44B, 46T, 46B, 47T, 48T, 48B, 49B, 50TL, 50TR, 51B, 52B, 53T, 55B, 56B, 57B, 60B, 61B, 62B, 64T, 64B, 65TL, 68T, 69C, 76B, 78T, 78C, 80B, 81TL, 81TR, 81BL, 83C, 85TR, 86B, 87T, 87B, 88T, 89B, 93C, 96CT, 96CB, 96B, 100T, 100B, 101T, 104C, 105B, 106TR, 106CB, 106B, 107CB
Rainbow Gardens: 40B, 107CT
Kenneth Rice: 1, 4–5, 7, 8, 9, 10, back cover
William Strode/Black Star: 15T, 32C

Front Cover
Top left: Palm: *Chrysalidocarpus lutescens*
Top center: Orchid: *Vanda*
Top right: *Monstera deliciosa*
Center left: *Saintpaulia* 'Granger's Wonderland'
Center: *Dieffenbachia* 'Tropic Snow'
Center right: *Notocactus leninghausii*
Bottom left: Bromeliad: *Aechmea fasciata*
Bottom center: Orchid: *Brassia*
Bottom right: *Asparagus densiflora* 'Sprengeri'

Title Page
Orchids add color to a hallway table arrangement.

Back Cover
A medicine plant (*Aloe vera*) thrives under this halogen light.

Ortho's Houseplant Encyclopedia

A Gallery
of Houseplants

Plants add warmth and tranquillity to a room, turning a house or apartment into a home. They keep us in touch with nature.

There are few things more appealing than a healthy, thriving plant. But keeping a plant healthy involves more than just placing it in a corner and watering it occasionally. Plants should be chosen to suit your home, your life-style, and your growing conditions.

The introduction presents the basics of plant care—the general needs of all plants for water, light, humidity, temperature, and fertilizer.

Most of the book is devoted to an encyclopedia detailing over 290 plants. The listings are divided into three categories—flowering plants, foliage plants, and cacti and succulents. Since many plants are not exclusively one or the other, you'll find them placed according to their most interesting feature. A few plants are listed in both the flowering and foliage plant sections.

Entries are in alphabetical order, by botanical name. Some plants are grouped by family and alphabetized under the family name. Beneath each botanical name the most familiar common names are listed.

For each entry, you'll find a general description of the plant as well as specific light, water, humidity, and temperature needs. You'll also find information on fertilizing, propagating, and grooming the plant, as well as tips on when to repot and any common problems. Use these care guides as a horticultural reference to help you select the plants that best suit you.

Dwarf anthurium (Anthurium schezeranum), Tillandsia, and a planter filled with Streptocarpus, guzmania, and ivy blend together into a pleasing display on this low table—while also drawing attention to the garden outside.

The Basics of Plant Care

To the beginning indoor gardener, caring for houseplants can be difficult at first. Watering, lighting, fertilizing, grooming, propagating, and seasonal care are initially bewildering, but they become easy and natural once you understand the basic process of plant growth.

The Parts of a Plant

There are four parts to most plants: roots, stems, leaves, and flowers. All are crucial to plant growth and health.

Roots anchor the plant and absorb the water and minerals that nourish it. They send water and nutrients to the stem, to start their journey to other parts of the plant. Roots of some plants also store food.

The stem transports water, minerals, and manufactured food to the leaves, buds, and flowers. It also physically supports the plant. Stems can store food during a plant's dormant period, and those of some plants can also manufacture food.

The leaf manufactures food for the plant through photosynthesis, absorbing light over its thin surface area. Its pores absorb and diffuse gases and water vapor during photosynthesis, respiration, and transpiration.

The flower is the sexual reproductive organ of the plant. Most plants flower in their natural environment, but only certain plants bloom indoors.

Photosynthesis, Respiration, and Transpiration

Plants harness the energy of the sun to manufacture their own food, in the form of sugar, through the process of photosynthesis. In photosynthesis, light energy, carbon dioxide, and water interact with the green plant pigment chlorophyll to produce plant sugars and oxygen, which is released into the atmosphere. The carbon dioxide is drawn from the atmosphere by the leaves, and the water is supplied by the roots.

In plant respiration, the sugar created by photosynthesis combines with oxygen to release energy. This energy is used for growth and survival and enables the plant to convert the building materials provided by nutrients in the soil into plant tissues.

Transpiration, the movement of water vapor from a leaf into the atmosphere, is important in stabilizing leaf temperatures (keeping them cool) in much the same way that human perspiration has a cooling effect. As water vapor leaves the plant through leaf pores (stomata), the leaf cools. The higher the temperature and the lower the humidity, the faster a plant transpires.

A mix of flowering and foliage plants adds the finishing touch to this elegant living room.

Watering Plants

Houseplants are container plants; their roots are confined to the container and cannot reach far for sustenance. Although watering sounds like an easy part of plant care, poor watering is responsible for killing more houseplants than anything else.

Contrary to popular opinion, overwatering is more often the culprit for a plant's water problems than underwatering. Since the roots cannot absorb more water than the plant needs, excess water, unless it drains away, will displace oxygen from the soil. This suffocates the roots and leads to rot. To avoid an overwatering problem, don't assume a plant needs more water when it doesn't grow as expected.

Experienced indoor gardeners never water by the calendar. The amount of water a plant needs varies with the species and its native habitat, the soil in which it is growing, and the light, temperature, and humidity in your home. Plants with a lot of leaf surface or soft, lush foliage will be thirstier than those with less foliage or waxy or leathery leaves.

Water needs are also affected by the growth cycle of the plant. A plant absorbs more water during active growth periods than

An unused fireplace is softened and highlighted by the ivy that surrounds the logs and fills in the space around them.

during rest periods. The size and the type of container is also important. In a small pot, moisture is absorbed quickly; too large a pot retains too much water. A plant in a porous clay pot needs water more frequently than one in a plastic or glazed pot.

The easiest way to find out when your plant needs water is to test by touch. Poke your finger into the soil to feel the degree of moisture. To double-check, rub a little soil between your thumb and index finger; the soil should feel dry to the touch to an inch below the surface, but not powdery. With a little experience, you'll be able to tell when the plant needs water. You can also use moisture meters, but the final determination should be how dry the soil feels and how a plant looks.

A plant that is wilting or drooping is thirsty—it needs water at once! Water a plant in this condition thoroughly, and try not to let this happen often—a plant that wilts again and again will not survive long.

Water Temperature
Plants prefer tepid water; cold water can harm roots or foliage and excessively hot water can kill a plant instantly. Let water from the

cold-water tap warm up to room temperature. If the water sits overnight, the dissolved chemicals present in tap water will evaporate.

How to Water

Watering plants in the morning allows any moisture left on the foliage to evaporate by evening; foliage that remains cool and wet is more prone to disease. Always water thoroughly, until the soil is saturated. If your plant receives only superficial waterings, its roots will grow toward the surface of the soil. It is better to water less often and more deeply.

The water should take only a minute or so to drain. If it takes more than 10 or 15 minutes, the drainage hole may be blocked. Poke a stick into the hole to loosen the compacted soil.

Don't let plants sit in water; if the plant is in a saucer, pour off any drained water within an hour. If the plant is too heavy to lift, use a turkey baster to remove the water.

When water drains through the pot rapidly, it may be running down between the rootball and the pot and not soaking in. This may happen after a plant has been allowed to dry out; it can be remedied by submerging the plant in water to the rim of its pot. Water will also run through a potbound plant without wetting the roots thoroughly. If you can't keep a plant moist, even when you are watering it every day, it may need a larger pot.

Baskets, Hiemalis begonias (Begonia × hiemalis), *and wax fruit form a three-dimensional still life on the shelf of an étagère.*

Lighting Plants

For plants, light means life. It is as essential to them as food is for humans. For that reason, it is important to study the available light before shopping for plants for a special spot.

There are five commonly used categories for defining plant light conditions. *Low light* is one in light shade, a position well back from the nearest window. There is enough light to read by without too much strain, but no direct sunlight.

Moderate light is average indoor light, neither sunny nor shady. A position directly in front of a north window or slightly back from an east or west one gets moderate light.

Bright, indirect light is an all-purpose light level at which both foliage and flowering plants thrive. It is found in a northeast or northwest window that receives a few hours of early morning or late afternoon sun and is well lit the rest of the day.

Direct sunlight is between two and five hours in the morning or afternoon, but not the full strength of the midday sun. Usually this is the light found directly in front of an east or west window or a few feet back from a south window.

More than four or five hours of direct sunlight daily is *full sun.* An unshaded window facing due south during the summer months receives full sun. Full sun is easily softened by installing sheer curtains or moving plants back several feet from an unshaded window.

A halogen lamp spotlights the dramatic form of this medicine plant (Aloe vera), providing exceptional light for its growth.

Humidity Levels

The moisture content of the air defines the term humidity. It is expressed as relative humidity; a percentage of the maximum amount of water vapor the air can hold at a given temperature. Nearly all houseplants grow best in a relative humidity of 50 percent or higher. Moisture-rich areas such as bathrooms and kitchens are more humid than other areas of the house.

Temperature Levels

In concert with light and humidity, temperature affects plant metabolism. Most indoor plants adapt to normal indoor temperatures (55° to 75° F). At night, they almost all benefit from at least a five degree drop in temperature, which gives them a chance to recover from any rapid water loss that may have taken place during the day.

Temperatures change with the seasons, even indoors. In winter, home heating and cold drafts from windows and doors can cause fluctuating temperatures; in summer, the temperature at a south-facing window can soar.

Fertilizing Plants

Photosynthesis provides plants with the sugar and other carbohydrates they need. Fertilizers provide the nutritive minerals they require for healthy growth. Plants that need to be fertilized exhibit slow growth, pale leaves, weak stems, small or nonexistent flowers, or dropped leaves.

Fertilizers come in many different formulations to suit various types of plants. The labels usually list three numbers; these are, in order, the percentages of nitrogen, phosphorous, and potassium that make up the fertilizer. In addition to these three nutrients, plants need three secondary nutrients—sulfur, calcium, and magnesium—and minute quantities of iron, zinc, manganese, copper, chlorine, boron, and molybdenum.

Fertilizers are available in many forms, and their strength varies widely. Before applying fertilizers, always read the label first and follow the directions carefully. Remember that more is not better. Excess fertilizer can burn roots and leaves.

In addition to the regular maintenance needs listed above, plants require further periodic care. This may include occasional grooming and repotting, as well as checking for any pests, diseases, or cultural problems. You may also want to reproduce your plant specimen, using a proven propagation method.

The gallery of houseplants that follows describes almost three hundred houseplants and their cultural needs. Use it to find just the right plants for your home.

Flowering Houseplants

Plants that produce beautiful flowers are extremely popular for indoor gardens. Care requirements for these plants may vary according to whether they are grown primarily for their flowers or for their foliage. The cultural information provided in this section promotes flowering.

Quite a few flowering houseplants are purchased as mature specimens already in bloom. Many of them are not well suited to being kept indoors after flowering, except in a greenhouse or solarium setting with a great deal of light, space, and humidity. These might be classified as plants used indoors while flowering. Some of the most common indoor plants, such as poinsettias, Easter lilies, and chrysanthemums, are in this category. In these cases, the care guides will help you to prolong the indoor life of a plant. The care guides generally describe the conditions necessary to keep the plants growing and bring them into bloom year after year.

Many bulbous plants that can be brought into flower indoors are included in this section of the gallery. Many bulbs can be placed almost anywhere indoors as decorative items when in bloom and then planted outdoors after flowering. Others need tending after flowering to initiate a dormancy period before they bloom again. Bulbous plants for flowering indoors are listed separately in the gallery. The individual care guides explain the requirements after flowering.

Abutilon hybridum

Abutilon
Abutilon, flowering-maple, Chinese-lantern

A tropical, viny shrub of the Hollyhock family, abutilon is extremely vigorous, growing several feet each year. Its bell-shaped flowers are striking, and its leaves, sometimes dappled with yellow or white, are shaped like a maple's. Its stems can be espaliered or trained onto a trellis.

The popularity of abutilon has spurred the development of hybrids with large blossoms in a wide range of colors. *A. hybridum* (Chinese-lantern) produces white, yellow, salmon, or purple blooms. *A. megapotamicum* 'Variegata' (trailing abutilon) features red and yellow blossoms with large, dark brown, pollen-bearing anthers. *A. pictum* 'Thompsonii' (formerly *A. striatum* 'Thompsonii') has an orange-salmon flower. Both *A. megapotamicum* 'Variegata' and *A. pictum* 'Thompsonii' have decorative yellow mottling on their leaves.

With bright, curtain-filtered light and moist soil, abutilon should grow rapidly and blossom most of the year. Fertilize monthly.

Light: Provide at least 4 hours of curtain-filtered sunlight from a bright south, east, or west window.

Water: Keep very moist, but do not allow to stand in water.

Humidity: Average indoor humidity levels.

Temperatures: 50° to 55° F at night, 65° to 70° F during the day.

Fertilization: Fertilize all year, more heavily in summer.

Propagation: Take cuttings from stems or shoots before they have hardened or matured.

Grooming: Because the plant grows so rapidly, pruning is a must for retaining its shape and size. Prune during the slow growth period in winter. Keep to desired height and shape with light pruning or clipping at any time.

Repotting: Repot in winter or early spring, as needed.

Problems: Dry soil or a high level of soluble salts may damage roots, causing plant to die back. If light is too low, plant will become spindly and weak.

Acalypha
Acalypha, copperleaf, beefsteak-plant, chenille-plant

Acalypha hispida is called the chenille-plant because its long plumes (more than 20 inches) of tiny, red flowers resemble chenille fringe. This plant blooms most heavily summer through fall, but will bloom the year around under good conditions. It needs light and warmth during blossoming. *A. wilkesiana* is usually grown for its distinctive leaves, which have red, copper, and pink tones that look like beefsteak. Winter flowers are tiny and not noteworthy. *A. repens*, a newer variety, is also becoming popular. Acalyphas are bushy plants that will get too big for indoor culture unless they are pruned several times a year.
Light: In winter, keep in direct sunlight for about 4 hours. In summer, provide curtain-filtered sunlight from a south or west window.
Water: Keep evenly moist. Water thoroughly and discard drainage.
Humidity: Average indoor humidity levels.
Temperatures: 55° to 60° F at night, 70° to 75° F during the day.
Fertilization: Fertilize only during late spring and summer months.
Propagation: Take cuttings from stems or shoots that have recently matured.
Grooming: Prune in early spring. Keep to desired height (2 or 3 feet is best) and shape with light pruning or clipping at any time. Give plant plenty of room.
Repotting: Repot infrequently. Plants need a large container for blooming and attaining proper form.
Problems: Leaves will drop if soil is too wet or too dry. If plant is in a draft or dry air, leaves will scorch.

Agapanthus
Agapanthus, blue African lily, lily-of-the-Nile

Agapanthuses are large plants, bearing clusters of lilylike blue or white flowers in summer. They bloom better when allowed to mature and get slightly pot bound. They need room and should not get too dry between waterings. The dwarf agapanthus (*A.* 'Peter Pan' and others) reaches a height of 8 to 12

inches and is well adapted to indoor growing. Most of the other species are approximately 2 feet tall.
Light: In winter, keep in direct sunlight for about 4 hours. In summer, provide curtain-filtered sunlight from a south or west window.
Water: Keep evenly moist. Water thoroughly and discard drainage.
Humidity: Average indoor humidity levels.
Temperatures: 50° to 55° F at night, 65° to 70° F during the day.
Fertilization: Fertilize only when plant is growing actively or flowering.
Propagation: Start new plants by dividing an old specimen. Seeds are available but can be more difficult than division.
Grooming: Pick off yellowed leaves.
Repotting: Repot infrequently.
Problems: Low light or soil that is too wet or too dry will cause leaves to yellow.

Allamanda
Allamanda, golden trumpet vine

Allamanda is a woody vine with large, fragrant, yellow blossoms in spring and summer. The plant needs warmth and lots of light. It will probably also need staking or training onto a trellis. *A. cathartica* is a vigorous climber that bears golden yellow flowers. It does well in a pot if vigorously pruned. Allamanda is occasionally available from specialist growers.
Light: Provide 4 hours or more of direct sunlight from a south window. Does best in a greenhouse setting.
Water: Keep evenly moist. Water thoroughly and discard drainage. In winter, keep plant a little drier, watering less frequently.
Humidity: Requires moist air. Use a humidifier for best results.
Temperatures: 55° to 60° F at night, 70° to 75° F during the day.
Fertilization: Fertilize only during late spring and summer months.
Propagation: Take cuttings from stems or shoots before they have hardened or matured.
Grooming: Pinch back new stem tips, being careful not to pinch off flower buds.
Repotting: New plants have to grow in a medium to large pot until almost root bound before they will bloom.

Acalypha hispida

Allamanda neriifolia

Agapanthus 'Peter Pan White'

Anthurium scherzeranum

Aphelandra squarrosa

Transplant into larger pots as needed.
Problems: Plant will not bloom if light is too low. In a draft or dry air, leaves will scorch. Susceptible to mealybugs.

Anthurium
Anthurium, flamingo-flower, tailflower

Anthuriums are among the best-known tropical flowers. Blossoms on *A. andraeanum* are long lasting and often used in weddings on Hawaii and other Pacific islands. They are popular in cut-flower arrangements around the world. The red or orange portion of the bloom is actually a bract (modified leaf); the tiny flowers appear on the spike, or spadix. New, everblooming varieties, such as 'Lady Jane' and 'Southern Blush', are now widely available.

Most anthuriums are large. *A. scherzeranum* is a small species, more suited for indoor or greenhouse culture. Keep anthuriums in humid air and fertilize them well when they are growing actively.

Light: Provide at least 4 hours of curtain-filtered sunlight from a bright south, east, or west window.
Water: Keep evenly moist. Water thoroughly and discard drainage.
Humidity: Requires moist air. Use a humidifier for best results.
Temperatures: 55° to 60° F at night, 70° to 75° F during the day.
Fertilization: Fertilize lightly throughout the growing season.
Propagation: Remove plantlets or rooted side shoots as they form.
Grooming: Mound up soil as high crowns form. Remove aerial roots.
Repotting: Leave room at the top to mound up soil as crown develops. Repot infrequently.
Problems: In a draft or dry air, leaves will scorch. Will not bloom if light is too low.

Aphelandra squarrosa
Aphelandra, zebra-plant

For 6 weeks in the fall, aphelandra provides an impressive, orderly display of color: large, conical, deep yellow flowers emerge from golden bracts. This small, evergreen shrub, a favorite of Victorian conservatories, also has unusual foliage—dark, elliptical leaves striped with ivory veins that create a zebra effect. The variety 'Louisae', the most

readily available cultivar, is compact with relatively small leaves. 'Apollo White' and 'Dania' are even more compact and produce leaves with striking vein patterns.

Aphelandra tends to become gangly. To combat this, cut it back after flowering, letting 1 or 2 pairs of leaves remain. Feed when the plant is growing actively or flowering, never allow the rootball to dry out, and keep the plant warm in winter.

Light: Place in a bright south, east, or west window with indirect sunlight.
Water: Keep very moist during growth and flowering; at other times keep evenly moist. Water thoroughly and discard drainage.
Humidity: Requires moist air. Use a humidifier for best results.
Temperatures: 55° to 60° F at night, 70° to 75° F during the day.
Fertilization: Fertilize only when plant is growing actively or flowering.
Propagation: Take cuttings from stems or shoots that have recently matured.
Grooming: Prune in early spring.
Repotting: Repot in winter or early spring, as needed.
Problems: If plant is in a draft or dry air, leaves will scorch. Leaves will drop if soil is too wet or too dry.

Ardisia
Ardisia, coralberry

Ardisias are woody ornamental shrubs that grow outdoors in warm climates. Their red berries at Christmastime make them particularly popular. The foliage is shiny and waxy, with small, fragrant, white or pink flowers. As indoor plants, they must have good light in winter. Cut them back severely in late winter, keeping them dry until they begin to grow. Keep only the strongest shoots, and train them to grow upward. Many gardeners place ardisias in shaded patio gardens during summer, to ensure better fruiting for the holidays.
Light: In winter, keep in direct sunlight for about 4 hours. In summer, provide curtain-filtered sunlight from a south or west window.
Water: Keep evenly moist. Water thoroughly and discard drainage.
Humidity: Requires moist air. Use a humidifier for best results.

Temperatures: 50° to 55° F at night, 60° to 65° F during the day.
Fertilization: Fertilize only during late spring and summer months.
Propagation: Take cuttings from stems or shoots before they have hardened or matured. Seeds are available, but can be more difficult than cuttings.
Grooming: Prune just before the heavy blossoming period, being careful not to cut off flower buds.
Repotting: Repot infrequently.
Problems: Susceptible to spider mites, especially if plant is dry, and to scale. If plant is in a draft or dry air, leaves will scorch. Dry soil or a high level of soluble salts may damage roots, causing plant to die back. Will not bloom if light is too low.

Azalea

See ***Rhododendron***.

Begonia

The begonia family contains more than 1,500 known species, offering a vast array of beautiful flowers, foliage shapes, and colors. Moreover, begonias are adaptable to almost any indoor environment. Many begonias are grown primarily for their foliage. This section describes some flowering varieties. Florists and garden centers offer many of these plants already in bloom for home decoration.

With a minimum of trouble, you should be able to keep your begonias healthy and blooming all year. In general, plenty of bright light, an average indoor temperature that drops slightly at night, and light applications of fertilizer will ensure constant blooms. Begonias are sensitive to overwatering, so take care to use soil that is rich in organic matter and drains well.

Begonia × cheimantha
Christmas begonia, Lorraine begonia

Begonia × cheimantha hybrids are popular because they bloom profusely in winter. They are bushy, dwarf plants, most frequently used in hanging baskets because the stems tend to arch outward attractively. Given enough light, Christmas begonias become covered with pink or white single flowers on long stems, or racemes. Since they bloom in winter, be sure to provide enough light and warmth and keep them evenly moist. After flowering, the plants become semidormant until late spring. Keep them drier during this period.
Light: Provide at least 4 hours of curtain-filtered sunlight from a bright south, east, or west window.
Water: Keep very moist during growth and flowering; at other times, allow to dry between waterings.
Humidity: Average indoor humidity levels.
Temperatures: 65° to 70° at night, 75° to 80° F during the day.
Fertilization: Fertilize only when plant is growing actively or flowering.
Propagation: Take stem cuttings at any time.
Grooming: Prune after flowering has ended, being careful not to remove flower buds.
Repotting: Cut back and repot when flowering stops.
Problems: Subject to crown rot in overly moist conditions. Leaves will drop if soil is too wet or too dry. Some varieties may get powdery mildew.

Begonia × hiemalis
Rieger begonia, hiemalis begonia, elatior begonia

Hiemalis begonias originated through hybridization of a winter-flowering begonia with hardy and vigorous tuberous begonias. Many varieties are available in florist shops. Hiemalis begonias are low growing and exceptionally bushy. Many are pendulous and are used in hanging baskets. Some of the newer cultivars have bronze or red foliage. The flowers are usually large and double; they come in yellow, red, white, and orange. Hiemalis begonias prefer cooler locations than most begonias, but do not like drafts. Give them plenty of light during their winter flowering period. These plants are hard to maintain through the summer and are often best treated as temporary flowering plants, to be discarded when blooming ceases.
Light: Provide at least 4 hours of curtain-filtered sunlight from a bright south, east, or west window.
Water: Keep evenly moist. Water thoroughly and discard drainage.
Humidity: Average indoor humidity levels.
Temperatures: 50° to 55° F at night, 65° to 70° F during the day.
Fertilization: Fertilize all year, more heavily in summer.

Begonia × hiemalis

Ardisia crispa

Begonia × semperflorens-cultorum

Bougainvillea 'Raspberry Ice'

Begonia × tuberhybrida 'Nonstop Orange'

Propagation: Take stem cuttings at any time.
Grooming: Pinch back new stem tips to improve form. Keep to desired height and shape with light pruning or clipping at any time. Be careful not to remove flower buds when pruning.
Repotting: Cut back and repot when flowering stops.
Problems: Subject to crown rot in overly moist conditions. Some cultivars are susceptible to powdery mildew.

Begonia × semperflorens-cultorum
Wax begonia, fibrous-rooted begonia

Wax begonias are the most popular of the fibrous-rooted begonia species. Many cultivars and hybrids exist. They are bushy plants with shiny, waxy, heart-shaped leaves. Given ample light, they bloom profusely in a variety of colors. Wax begonias are most commonly used as outdoor bedding annuals or in hanging baskets for patio gardens. However, they will flourish indoors with light fertilization, good light, and sufficient warmth.
Light: Provide at least 4 hours of curtain-filtered sunlight from a bright south, east, or west window.
Water: Keep evenly moist. Water thoroughly and discard drainage.
Humidity: Requires moist air. Use a humidifier for best results.
Temperatures: 65° to 70° F at night, 75° to 80° F during the day.
Fertilization: Fertilize lightly throughout the growing season.
Propagation: Take stem cuttings at any time. Seeds are available, but can be more difficult than cuttings.
Grooming: Pinch back new stem tips to improve form. Keep plant to desired height and shape with light pruning or clipping at any time. Be careful not to remove flower buds when pruning.
Repotting: Cut back and repot when flowering stops.
Problems: Subject to crown rot in overly moist conditions. If plant is in a draft or dry air, leaves will scorch. If light is too low, plant will get spindly and weak. Watch for mealybugs and powdery mildew.

Begonia × tuberhybrida
Tuberous begonia

Cultivars of tuberous begonias produce the largest flowers of all begonias grown indoors. Most are large plants that need good light, cool temperatures, and moist soil and air. It is best to buy a mature tuber, plant it, enjoy a flowering period, and then discard it or place it in the garden. Older plants tend to get spindly and weak indoors.
Light: Provide at least 4 hours of direct sunlight in winter. Provide curtain-filtered sunlight in summer, from a south or west window.
Water: Keep very moist at all times, but do not allow to stand in water.
Humidity: Use a humidifier for best results.
Temperatures: 50° to 55° F at night, 60° to 65° F during the day.
Fertilization: Fertilize lightly. Do not fertilize when in flower.
Propagation: Start new plants from the bulblets that develop beside the parent.
Grooming: Discard after flowering.
Repotting: Not usually done.
Problems: Subject to crown rot in overly moist conditions. Leaves will scorch if plant is in a draft or dry air.

Bougainvillea glabra
Bougainvillea

Bougainvilleas are among the most popular and most beautiful flowering shrubs in warm climates. Indoors, they must be pruned and trained to be manageable. They will probably not bloom in winter unless they are in a warm greenhouse. These plants can sometimes be purchased from a florist.
Light: Does best in a greenhouse setting.
Water: Let plant approach dryness before watering, then water thoroughly and discard drainage.
Humidity: Requires moist air. Use a humidifier for best results.
Temperatures: 55° to 60° F at night, 70° to 75° F during the day.
Fertilization: Fertilize only during late spring and summer months.
Propagation: Take cuttings from stems or shoots before they have hardened or matured. Seeds are available, but can be more difficult than cuttings. Root cuttings are another option.

Grooming: Prune after flowering.
Repotting: Repot in winter or early spring, as needed.
Problems: Will not bloom if light is too low. Poor drainage, too-frequent watering, or standing in water will cause root rot. Susceptible to mealybugs.

Bromeliads

Many gardeners have discovered that although bromeliads have exotic tropical foliage and flowers, they are not difficult to grow indoors. The most distinctive feature of bromeliads is the cup-shaped rosette of leaves, which holds the water that nourishes the plant. In some varieties, flowers and large, colorful bracts emerge from the center, creating a spectacular display. The bracts are modified leaves that grow from the same axils as the flowers. Originating in the tropics, most bromeliads are epiphytes (air plants). They grow suspended in trees and on rocks in their native habitat, gathering moisture and nutrients from rainfall and particles in the air.

Bromeliads are available in flower in many florist shops and garden centers. Display them in pots or hanging baskets, or attach them to boards. If you decide to keep them in pots, use a light soil that drains easily and pots that look a little small. Too-large containers and overwatering can be fatal to their small root system. When growing these plants in a pot, water mainly by filling the rosette, but don't forget to moisten the potting mix occasionally as well. Bromeliads need lots of sun and high temperatures to bloom. If you're having trouble inducing a bromeliad to flower, place it in a plastic bag with a ripe apple for a few days. The ethylene gas from the apple will initiate flower buds. When the plant stops flowering, the rosette starts to die, a slow process that can last as long as 3 years. Planting the offsets that form at the base of the plant will give you a collection that blooms year after year.

There are more than 2,000 bromeliad species. Some are grown for their flowers, others for their foliage. The following are particularly suitable for an indoor garden.

Aechmea
Living-vaseplant, urnplant, coralberry

The most common aechmea is *Aechmea fasciata* (living-vaseplant, urnplant). Its broad, thick leaves are mottled with gray and sea-green stripes and its conical rosette of pink bracts and large, dark blue flowers creates a splendid effect. An upright rosette of thick, silver-banded leaves distinguishes the striking *A. chantinii.* Its flowers last for several months.

A. fulgens discolor, commonly known as the coralberry, has broad leaves that are green on top and purple underneath. The contrast in the foliage is heightened by the purple flower. Red berries form after the flower dies.

Ananas comosus
Pineapple, ivory pineapple

If you know what a pineapple is, then you know an ananas. Pineapples are the fruit of *A. comosus.* You can grow one by cutting off a piece of the fruit along with the tuft (the crown of leaves at the top of the plant), planting it in a pot of soil, and placing it in full sun. Narrow, gray-green leaves with prickly ribbing on the side will form a striking rosette. The pineapple fruit will spring from the center for an unusual display, but this will happen only after several years. *A. comosus* 'Variegatus' (ivory pineapple) has the more attractive foliage.

Billbergia
Vaseplant, queen's-tears

Vaseplants are among the easiest bromeliads to grow, but they flower for only a short time. *B. nutans* (queen's-tears) has grassy, gray-green leaves and an arching spray of pink and green flowers. *B. pyramidalis* and *B. pyramidalis striata* sport long, green, strap leaves, bright red bracts tipped with violet, and upright, scarlet flowers with yellow stamens.

Cryptanthus
Earthstar, starfish-plant, rainbow-star

Called earthstars because of the shape of their rosettes, these plants are small and show great variation in leaf color, making them attractive plants for small spaces or dish gardens. *C. acaulis* (starfish-plant) has small, wavy-edged leaves in varying shades of yellow and green.

Bromeliad: *Aechmea fasciata*

Bromeliad: *Ananas comosus*

Bromeliad: *Billbergia vittata*

Bromeliad: *Dyckia fosterana*

Bromeliad: *Guzmania lingulata*

Bromeliad: *Neoregelia*
Bromeliad: *Cryptanthus*

Bromeliad: *Nidularium procerum*

C. bromelioides tricolor (rainbow-star) displays a colorful array of stripes down the length of its wavy leaves. *C. zonatus* (zebra-plant) resembles zebra skin, banded in ivory and shades of brown. *C. bivittatus* has green leaves with creamy white stripes. Some of the common hybrids of *C. bivittatus* include 'Starlite', 'It', and 'Pink Starlite'.

Dyckia species
Dyckia

Dyckias are slow-growing, medium-sized bromeliads with dark green, spiny foliage. In bright light during summer, the plants will produce orange flowers on spikes. One popular species is *D. brevifolia.*

Guzmania
Guzmania

The vase-shaped rosettes of guzmanias can grow to 20 inches wide. They bloom from late winter to summer, depending on the species. The true flowers are small but are surrounded by large, showy bracts in reds, yellows, or oranges. *G. lingulata,* a popular species, has brightly colored bracts ranging from red to yellow, and white flowers.

Neoregelia
Blushing bromeliad,
painted-fingernail-plant

Neoregelias produce large rosettes of thick, shiny leaves. When mature, *N. carolinae* 'Tricolor' (blushing bromeliad) reaches a diameter of 30 inches. Lightly toothed leaves, variegated in cream and green, jut out in an orderly pattern. Just before flowering, the young leaves in the center turn bright red. *N. spectabilis* features green leaves with pink-tipped ends, inspiring the name *painted-fingernail-plant.*

Nidularium
Bird's-nest bromeliad

The center of the leaf rosette of nidulariums changes color many weeks before the flowers appear. Various species are available with foliage of different shades and patterns. Among the most popular is *N. innocentii,* with its small, red leaves that cradle white flowers at the center. The plants will tolerate moderate light, but may bloom only in bright light.

Tillandsia
Tillandsia, air plant, Spanish moss

Many species of tillandsias are available to indoor gardeners. Even the *T. usneoides* (Spanish moss) commonly seen as an epiphyte in the South is occasionally grown indoors. Most tillandsias have narrow, arching foliage, either like grass leaves or palm leaves. Some of the smaller species are popular as hanging plants or dish-garden plants. Sword-shaped flower spikes appear in summer. *T. cyanea* has a rosette of bright green leaves, deep pink or red bracts, and violet blue flowers. *T. ionantha* has miniature silver gray leaves and violet flowers.

Vriesea
Vriesea, flaming-sword

The genus *Vriesea* features many plants attractive for both their foliage and flowers. *V. splendens*, a popular variety, forms a rosette of wide, purple-banded leaves. The common name, flaming-sword, refers to the flower, a long spike of red bracts and yellow flowers. The bloom will last for several weeks.

Care of Bromeliads

Light: Abundant light. An east or west window is best. Ananas and Dyckia require full sun.
Water: Always keep the cup of rosette-type bromeliads filled with water (preferably rainwater), changing it occasionally. Allow plants growing in pots to dry out, then water lightly so that they are barely moist. Overwatering and poor drainage will kill bromeliads. Spray epiphytic bromeliads not growing in pots with warm water regularly.
Humidity: Dry air is generally not harmful.
Temperatures: Average constant temperatures of 65° to 70° F are fine for foliage types and plants in flower. Warmer temperatures (75° to 80° F) are needed to initiate flower buds.
Fertilization: Fertilize lightly once a year, in early spring.
Propagation: Remove mature offsets and a sizable section of roots from large plants and pot shallowly in light soil. Keep warm.
Grooming: Wash leaves occasionally.

Repotting: Rarely necessary.
Problems: Brown areas on leaves usually indicate sunburn; move plant out of direct sunlight. Brown tips on leaves result from dry air. Watch for scale and mealybugs on foliage and flowers.

Browallia
Browallia, sapphire-flower

Browallia is a woody plant usually grown in a hanging basket, since its shoots tend to spread and trail. In a regular pot, it will need pruning and staking. Given enough light, the plant will bear blue or white, medium-sized flowers all year. In winter, keep it watered with room-temperature water and continue to fertilize it lightly until it has finished flowering.
Light: In winter, keep in about 4 hours of direct sunlight. In summer, provide curtain-filtered sunlight from a south or west window.
Water: Keep very moist at all times, but do not allow to stand in water.
Humidity: Requires moist air. Use a humidifier for best results.
Temperatures: 55° to 60° F at night, 70° to 75° F during the day.
Fertilization: Fertilize all year, more heavily in summer.
Propagation: Start from seeds. Sow in a small pot and transplant seedlings as needed. Or take cuttings from stems or shoots that have recently matured.
Grooming: Prune after flowering.
Repotting: Repot each year, in early summer, for best growth.
Problems: If plant is in a draft or dry air, leaves will scorch. Will not bloom if light is too low. Susceptible to whiteflies.

Brunfelsia
Yesterday-today-and-tomorrow

The common name for brunfelsia comes from the fact that as it ages, its flowers change from dark purple to almost white. The mildly fragrant, medium-sized flowers grow in clusters almost all year long if they have plenty of light. They need a moderate rest period in late spring.
Light: In winter, keep in direct sunlight for about 4 hours. In summer, provide curtain-filtered sunlight from a south or west window.

Bromeliad: *Tillandsia cyanea*

Bromeliad: *Vriesea splendens*
Browallia speciosa 'Major'

Brunfelsia pauciflora var. calycina

Calliandra haematocephala
Calceolaria crenatiflora

Water: Keep very moist during growth and flowering; at other times, allow to dry between waterings.
Humidity: Average indoor humidity levels.
Temperatures: 50° to 55° F at night, 65° to 70° F during the day.
Fertilization: Fertilize only when plant is growing actively or flowering.
Propagation: Take cuttings from stems or shoots before they have hardened or matured.
Grooming: Prune well in early spring. Pinch back new stem tips to improve form. Be careful not to destroy flower buds when pruning.
Repotting: Cut back and repot when flowering stops.
Problems: Will get spindly and weak if light is too low. Dry soil or high level of soluble salts may damage roots, causing plant to die back.

Calceolaria crenatiflora
Calceolaria, pocketbook-flower, slipper-flower

The intricate flowers of calceolaria (often sold as *Calceolaria herbeohybrida*) are shaped like a sac. Cultivars come in many colors, including red, pink, maroon, and yellow. Most have purple or brown markings on the petals. The plants are difficult to grow from seeds because they are sensitive to improper watering and fertilizing. They like cool nights and are suited to a small greenhouse or window box. Before they flower, pinch back stems to train them into bushy plants.
Light: Blooming plants can be placed anywhere. Growing plants need curtain-filtered sunlight in summer and direct sunlight in winter.
Water: Keep evenly moist. Water thoroughly and discard drainage.
Humidity: Requires moist air. Use a humidifier for best results.
Temperatures: 40° to 45° F at night, 60° to 65° F during the day.
Fertilization: Fertilize lightly throughout the growing season. Do not fertilize blooming plants.
Propagation: Start from seeds. Sow in a small pot and transplant seedlings as needed.
Grooming: Pinch back new stem tips to improve form, stopping when the flowering period approaches. Discard after flowering.

Repotting: Transplant seedlings several times, as they grow.
Problems: Subject to crown rot if planted deeply, watered over the crown, or watered late in the day. If plant is in a draft or dry air, leaves will scorch. Susceptible to whiteflies.

Calliandra
Calliandra, powder-puff, flame bush

Given lots of sunlight, calliandras will produce large, red, or pink flower heads with many stamens, resembling powder puffs. They are winter-flowering, bushy shrubs. Their compound leaves are like the honeylocust's. Calliandras will get quite large and should be pruned to a height of 3 feet. Because they need warmth and light, they are best suited for greenhouses or solariums. Usually available only from specialist nurseries.
Light: Provide 4 hours or more of direct sunlight from a south window. Does best in a greenhouse setting.
Water: Let plant approach dryness before watering, then water thoroughly and discard drainage.
Humidity: Requires moist air. Use a humidifier for best results.
Temperatures: 65° to 70° F at night, 75° to 80° F during the day.
Fertilization: Fertilize only during late spring and summer.
Propagation: Take cuttings from stems or shoots that have recently matured.
Grooming: Prune in early spring. Keep to desired height and shape with light pruning or clipping at any time.
Repotting: Repot in winter or early spring, as needed.
Problems: Will get spindly and weak if light is too low.

Camellia
Camellia

Camellias are evergreen shrubs with dark green, glossy leaves. In spring they produce large, fragrant flowers in shades of white, pink, or red. *C. japonica,* a species commonly grown indoors, has more than 2,000 cultivars in a variety of colors, sizes, and shapes.

This is basically a plant for cool greenhouses or outdoor use in moderate climates; it requires a set of exacting conditions to succeed indoors. A cool

room with good air circulation is a must. When buds appear in winter or spring, do not move the plant, and guard against fluctuations in temperature and soil moisture or the buds will drop.
Light: Keep in about 4 hours of direct sunlight in winter. Provide curtain-filtered sunlight in summer, from a south or west window.
Water: Keep evenly moist. Water thoroughly and discard drainage.
Humidity: Average indoor humidity levels.
Temperatures: 40° to 45° F at night, 60° to 65° F during the day.
Fertilization: Use an acid-based fertilizer during late spring and summer, and add trace elements once in spring.
Propagation: Take cuttings from stems or shoots that have recently matured.
Grooming: Prune after flowering. Pinch back new stem tips to improve form. Be careful not to remove flower buds when pruning.
Repotting: Repot infrequently.
Problems: If plant is in a draft or dry air, leaves will scorch. Leaves will drop if soil is too wet or too dry. Somewhat susceptible to mealybugs and, to a lesser degree, to scale.

Campanula
Campanula, star-of-Bethlehem, bellflower

Campanulas are small, bushy plants that bear an abundance of flowers from August through November. The flowers are purple, blue, or white, and many species have bell-like flowers, giving the plant one of its common names. *C. isophylla* and *C. isophylla* 'Alba' have heart-shaped leaves and hanging stems up to 2 feet long. Many indoor gardeners prefer to plant campanula in a small hanging basket.
Light: Keep in about 4 hours of direct sunlight in winter. Provide curtain-filtered sunlight in summer, from a south or west window.
Water: Keep very moist during growth and flowering; at other times, allow to dry between waterings.
Humidity: Average indoor humidity levels.
Temperatures: 50° to 55° F at night, 65° to 70° F during the day.
Fertilization: Fertilize only during late spring and summer.

Propagation: Take cuttings from stems or shoots before they have hardened or matured.
Grooming: Cut back in late fall or early winter, as needed. Pinch back new stem tips for 6 to 8 weeks to improve form, being careful not to remove flower buds.
Repotting: Repot in winter or early spring, as needed.
Problems: If plant is in a draft or dry air, leaves will scorch. Poor drainage, too-frequent watering, or standing in water will cause root rot. Subject to crown rot in overly moist conditions.

Capsicum
Ornamental pepper

Ornamental peppers are not particularly noteworthy until they become loaded with fruit in late summer and fall. Since it takes very good light to accomplish heavy blossoming and fruit set, ornamental peppers are best suited for greenhouse culture. The fruit changes from green to yellow to its final coloration—usually bright red—as it matures. Even small plants set fruit. They make attractive tabletop or windowsill decorations. The fruit is edible, but being a chili pepper, it is extremely hot. Keep away from small children.
Light: Provide 4 hours or more of direct sunlight from a south window. Does best in a greenhouse setting.
Water: Keep evenly moist. Water thoroughly and discard drainage.
Humidity: Average indoor humidity levels.
Temperatures: 55° to 60° F at night, 70° to 75° F during the day.
Fertilization: Fertilize only when plant is growing actively or flowering.
Propagation: Start from seeds. Sow in a small pot and transplant seedlings as needed.
Grooming: Prune in spring. Pinch out new stem tips to improve form. Be careful not to remove flower buds when pruning. Discard after fruiting.
Repotting: Repot in winter or early spring, as needed.
Problems: Will not bloom if light is too low. Leaves will drop if soil is too wet or too dry. Susceptible to aphids and spider mites.

Camellia japonica 'Debutant'

Campanula isophylla
Capsicum annuum

Carissa macrocarpa

Carissa macrocarpa
Natal plum

Dwarf cultivars of Natal plum (sometimes sold as *Carissa grandiflora*) do well in greenhouses or solariums and are popular indoor bonsai subjects. They produce abundant foliage on woody stems. Their large, white flowers are fragrant and are followed by red, plumlike fruits. These are edible, but have a bitter, cranberry taste. Fruit and blossoms appear together on the plant at certain times of the year. Keep Natal plums pruned to between 2 and 3 feet to prevent legginess. Though you may find the plant in outdoor nurseries in the South, it is usually available only from specialty growers elsewhere.

Light: Provide 4 hours or more of direct sunlight from a south window. Does best in a greenhouse setting.

Water: Keep evenly moist. Water thoroughly and discard drainage.

Humidity: Average indoor humidity levels.

Temperatures: 55° to 60° F at night, 70° to 75° F during the day.

Fertilization: Fertilize lightly throughout the growing season.

Propagation: Take stem cuttings at any time.

Grooming: Keep to desired height and shape with light pruning or clipping at any time.

Repotting: Repot in winter or early spring, as needed.

Problems: Will get spindly and weak if light is too low.

Chrysanthemum frutescens
Marguerite, Boston daisy, Paris daisy

Marguerites are vigorous growers that produce yellow or white flowers intermittently throughout the year. Their lacy foliage has a distinctive aroma. The plants need lots of light to grow indoors. They tend to look rangy if not clipped. Keep them well branched and approximately 12 inches tall. Replace them when they get weak and spindly.

Light: Provide 4 hours or more of direct sunlight from a south window. Does best in a greenhouse setting.

Water: Keep evenly moist. Water thoroughly and discard drainage.

Humidity: Average indoor humidity levels.

Temperatures: 40° to 45° F at night, 60° to 65° F during the day.

Fertilization: Fertilize all year, more heavily in summer.

Propagation: Take stem cuttings at any time.

Grooming: Pinch back new stem tips to improve form, being careful not to remove flower buds. Start new plants to replace old specimens when they get weak.

Repotting: Repot at any time.

Problems: Spider mites can be a problem, especially if plant is too dry. Will not bloom, and will get spindly and weak, if light is too low.

Chrysanthemum × morifolium
Florist's chrysanthemum, florist's mum

Greenhouse hybrid chrysanthemums, or florist's chrysanthemums, are often given as gifts. They are considered houseplants because they are usually purchased while blooming, for display indoors. They can be transplanted into the garden, but are difficult to grow outdoors. Think of florist's mums as cut flowers that last a long time.

Commercial growers apply dwarfing chemicals to the plants and ensure year-round production by placing them in the dark to induce flowering during the long days of spring and summer. The large flowers come in every color of bloom except blue.

Look for plants with a few open blossoms and plenty of buds. Place the plant in a cool room on a windowsill where it will receive about 4 hours of direct sun daily. Morning or evening sun is best. It should bloom for 6 to 8 weeks.

Florist's mums are usually discarded after flowering, but if you want to save the plant, prune it back and reduce watering; then plant it in the garden. Without growth retardants, it will probably become quite leggy. Pinch it back often to maintain a full, bushy plant. Florist's mums are not hardy in cold climates and need to be indoors in a cold but frost-free room for winter.

Light: Place in a bright south, east, or west window.

Water: Keep evenly moist. Water thoroughly and discard drainage.

Humidity: Average indoor humidity levels.

Temperatures: 50° to 55° F at night, 60° to 65° F during the day.

Chrysanthemum frutescens

Chrysanthemum × morifolium

Fertilization: Do not fertilize when in flower. Fertilize lightly at other times.
Propagation: Take cuttings from stems or shoots before they have hardened or matured.
Grooming: Discard after flowering.
Repotting: Not usually done.
Problems: Spider mites can be a problem, especially if plant is too dry.

Citrus
Citrus

Plants in the citrus family have something for all seasons: shiny, dark green foliage; attractively scented, white flowers that appear intermittently throughout the year; and colorful, long-lasting fruits. The latter range in color from green to yellow or orange, depending on the species and the maturity of the fruit. Often fruits at various stages of development and color are found on the plant at the same time. All citrus are shrubby plants that normally become large with time, but they can be kept in check with regular pruning. Avoid trimming off branches with flowers or buds if you want a crop of fruit. Some citrus bear numerous thorns; others are mostly or entirely thornless.

Citrus fruits produced indoors tend to be sour or bitter and cannot be eaten fresh. They can, however, be used in any recipe that calls for citrus: marmalades, candies, and so on. To ensure fruit production indoors, pass from flower to flower, dusting each with a small paintbrush.

Growing citrus from store-bought fruit is a popular pastime. Sow the seeds in small pots in a moist growing medium, and cover with plastic wrap. Place the pot in a warm, brightly lit spot. The seedlings will appear in 2 or 3 weeks and become attractive, long-lived foliage plants. It is unlikely that plants raised from store-bought fruit will ever flower or produce fruit indoors, as the parent plants were selected for outdoor conditions. For good fruit production, start new plants from stem cuttings of selections that do bloom well indoors or buy plants that are already in bloom. The latter can be expensive, but they give quick results; young plants can be years away from flowering.

The best choice for indoor growing is × *Citrofortunella mitis,* actually a cross between *Citrus reticulata* (mandarin orange) and the closely related genus *Fortunella* (calamondin or miniature orange) so commonly seen in garden centers and florist shops. It blooms and produces fruit the year around. It also remains nicely compact with only minimal pruning. *Citrus limon* 'Meyer' (meyer lemon) is also productive indoors, bearing yellow fruits identical to store-bought lemons. *C. limon* 'Ponderosa' (ponderosa lemon), another good choice, produces enormous fruits with a thick, rough skin, usually only one or two at a time. Occasionally, *C. sinensis* cultivars (sweet oranges) are also offered. They require ideal conditions to produce fruit indoors. Another citrus worth noting is *Fortunella margarita* (kumquat), which produces small, orange-yellow, oblong fruits.
Light: Provide 4 hours or more of direct sunlight from a south window. Does best in a greenhouse setting.
Water: Let plant approach dryness before watering; then water thoroughly and discard drainage each time.
Humidity: Average indoor humidity levels.
Temperatures: 50° to 55° F at night, 65° to 70° F during the day.
Fertilization: Use an acid-based fertilizer. Add trace elements once a year, in spring.
Propagation: Take stem cuttings at any time.
Grooming: Keep to desired height and shape with light pruning or clipping at any time.
Repotting: Repot infrequently.
Problems: Will not bloom if light is too low. Leaves will drop if soil is too wet or too dry. Subject to infestations of mealybugs, scale, and spider mites. Lack of trace elements (particularly iron) may cause leaf yellowing.

Clerodendrum
Clerodendrum, glorybower, bleeding-heart

Clerodendrums are actually woody shrubs that get quite large when growing outdoors. The most popular cultivar is *C. thomsoniae,* which inspired the name "bleeding-heart" because of its beautiful and intricate white and red flowers. It is often found in florist shops. The flowers cluster on trailing stems, so the plant is commonly used in

Citrus limon 'Lisbon'

Fortunella margarita 'Nagami'
Citrus × *limonia* 'Rangpoor'

Clerodendrum thomsoniae

Clivia miniata
Crinum 'Cape Dawn'

hanging baskets. Keep clerodendrums warm and give them plenty of room.
Light: Provide at least 4 hours of curtain-filtered sunlight from a bright south, east, or west window.
Water: Keep very moist during growth and flowering; at other times, allow to dry between waterings.
Humidity: Average indoor humidity levels.
Temperatures: 55° to 60° F at night, 70° to 75° F during the day.
Fertilization: Fertilize only during late spring and summer.
Propagation: Take cuttings from stems or shoots before they have hardened or matured.
Grooming: Prune after flowering. Pinch back new stem tips to improve form. Be careful not to remove flower buds when pruning.
Repotting: Repot infrequently.
Problems: Spider mites can be a problem, especially if plant gets too dry. Also susceptible to mealybugs. Poor drainage, too-frequent watering, or standing in water will cause root rot.

Clivia miniata
Kaffir-lily

A herbaceous plant, *Clivia miniata* is a member of the amaryllis family and is named after Charlotte Clive, Duchess of Northumberland, who developed it in 1866 as an indoor plant. Thick stems 12 to 15 inches long emerge from a crown of leathery, strap leaves and support large clusters of orange, trumpet-shaped flowers with yellow throats. French and Belgian hybrids bloom in yellow to deep red-orange. After flowers fade in late spring, ornamental red berries form and add a touch of lasting color.

This winter bloomer does well in a room that receives plenty of indirect sunlight and cools down during the night. Houses in cold climates are most suitable. Crowded roots that are left undisturbed for years produce the best blooms; repotting is rarely necessary.
Light: Provide at least 4 hours of curtain-filtered sunlight from a bright south, east, or west window.
Water: Keep very moist during growth and flowering; at other times, allow to dry between waterings.
Humidity: Average indoor humidity levels.

Temperatures: 50° to 55° F at night, 60° to 65° F during the day in fall and winter. Normal room temperatures are fine during spring and summer.
Fertilization: Fertilize only when plant is growing actively or flowering. During fall the plant rests; apply no fertilizer and reduce water. From January to August, fertilize monthly.
Propagation: Start new plants from the plantlets that develop beside the parent bulb.
Grooming: Pick off yellowed leaves. Cut flower stalks if you wish.
Repotting: Repot infrequently.
Problems: Subject to crown rot if planted deeply, watered over the crown, or watered late in the day.

Crinum
Crinum, Bengal lily, milk-and-wine-lily

Crinums are one of the largest bulb plants grown indoors. The pink, red, or white flowers are fragrant and sometimes 6 inches across. They are borne in clusters on top of a 3-foot stalk. The leaves are narrow and 4 feet long. Crinum is a magnificent plant, and needs a lot of room. It flowers indoors in spring and summer, although it can also bloom in autumn. Keep it well lit, moist, and fertilized from spring until October, and give it a moderately dry resting period during winter.
Light: Provide curtain-filtered sunlight in summer, from a south or a west window.
Water: Keep very moist during growth and flowering; at other times, allow to dry between waterings.
Humidity: Average indoor humidity levels.
Temperatures: 50° to 55° F at night, 65° to 70° F during the day.
Fertilization: Fertilize only when plant is growing actively or flowering.
Propagation: Start new plants from the bulblets that develop beside the parent bulb.
Grooming: Remove old leaves as plant goes dormant. Cut flower stalks after blooming if you wish. Give plant plenty of room.
Repotting: Repot infrequently.
Problems: No significant problems.

Crocus
Crocus

Crocuses, because of their small size, make an excellent midwinter-flowering pot plant. Florists often sell them in bloom in winter. Since the plants usually grow only a few inches tall, they look best in a broad, shallow pot, planted in clumps. Crocuses are available in many colors and shades. The corms must be given a cold (35° F) treatment in the pot before forcing. Many indoor gardeners pot newly purchased mature corms in October, place them in a cool (not freezing) place until January, and then bring them inside for flowering. After the foliage has died back, place the plants in the garden or discard.

Light: Place in a bright, indirectly lit south, east, or west window.

Water: Keep evenly moist. Water thoroughly and discard drainage.

Humidity: Average indoor humidity levels.

Temperatures: 40° to 45° F at night, 60° to 65° F during the day.

Fertilization: Do not fertilize when plant is in flower. Fertilize lightly at other times.

Propagation: Start new plants from the bulblets that develop beside the parent bulb. It will take several years to get a new corm to blooming size.

Grooming: Remove flowers as they fade. Discard after flowering.

Repotting: None needed.

Problems: No significant problems.

Crossandra infundibuliformis
Crossandra, firecracker-flower

Given ample light and fertilizer, crossandras will bloom almost continuously. The flowers appear on short stalks at the ends of growing shoots, overlapping one another. They are bright salmon red. Cut them back as needed to maintain shape. Discard them when they get leggy or pot bound.

Light: Provide 4 hours of direct sunlight in winter. Provide curtain-filtered sunlight in summer, from a south or west window.

Water: Keep evenly moist. Water thoroughly and discard drainage.

Humidity: Requires moist air. Use a humidifier for best results.

Temperatures: 55° to 60° F at night, 70° to 75° F during the day.

Crocus vernus

Crossandra infundibuliformis

Cuphea hyssopifolia

Cuphea ignea

Cyclamen persicum

Fertilization: Fertilize all year, more heavily in summer.

Propagation: Start from seeds. Sow in a small pot and transplant seedlings as needed. Or, take stem cuttings at any time.

Grooming: Keep to desired height and shape with light pruning or clipping at any time. Start new plants to replace old specimens when they get weak or old.

Repotting: Transplant seedlings several times, as they grow.

Problems: Poor drainage, too-frequent watering, or standing in water will cause root rot.

Cuphea
Cigarplant, elfin-herb, Hawaiian heather

Two quite different cupheas are grown as houseplants. The elfin-herb, also known as Hawaiian heather (*Cuphea hyssopifolia*), bears bell-shaped, six-petaled flowers, usually pink but also purple or white, and has needlelike leaves. It is commonly grown as an indoor bonsai. The cigarplant (*C. ignea,* sometimes labeled *C. platycentra*) bears red, tubular flowers with a white tip that resemble a burning cigar, giving it its common name. Its leaves are small and broad. Both are bushy plants that require some pruning to maintain their shape. Given good light, they will grow well and flower at any season.

Light: Provide 4 hours or more of direct sunlight in winter; provide bright, indirect light the rest of the year. Attractive plant for light gardens.

Water: Keep evenly moist. Water thoroughly and discard drainage.

Humidity: Cigarplant requires moist air; use a humidifier for best results. Elfin-herb or Hawaiian heather tolerates average indoor humidity levels.

Temperatures: 55° to 65° F at night, 70° to 75° F during the day.

Fertilization: Fertilize when plant is growing actively.

Propagation: Take stem cuttings at any time. Cigarplant is also readily grown from seed. Start in February for summer flowering, and again in July for winter blossoms.

Grooming: Prune and pinch as needed. Cigarplant is usually discarded after blooming.

Repotting: Can be repotted at any time. Grow in small pots for plentiful flowers. Transplant seedlings several times, as they grow.

Problems: Will not bloom in low light.

Cyclamen persicum
Cyclamen

The heart-shaped, dark green leaves of cyclamen surround upright stems that are topped with butterfly blossoms from midautumn until midspring. Of the 15 species in the genus, *C. persicum* is most commonly grown indoors and is readily available from florists. Purchase plants in early fall when the blooming season begins for indoor color.

Cyclamen does best in a cool room with good air circulation but no drafts. When blooming, it needs as much sun as possible. Fertilize every 2 weeks.

Many people discard cyclamen after blooming, but the plants can be kept if they are given special care. When blooming ceases and the foliage dies back, put the plant in a cool spot and let the soil dry. In midsummer repot the corm with new soil in a small pot, and place it in a warm area to encourage root growth. As the plant grows, gradually return it to a cool location (55° F) to induce blooming.

Light: Place in a bright, indirectly lit south, east, or west window.

Water: Keep evenly moist. Water thoroughly from the bottom and discard drainage.

Humidity: Average indoor humidity levels.

Temperatures: 50° to 55° F at night, 60° to 65° F during the day.

Fertilization: Fertilize only when plant is growing actively or flowering.

Propagation: Start from seeds. Sow in a small pot and transplant seedlings as needed. It may take 2 years to get a blooming plant.

Grooming: Pick off yellowed leaves.

Repotting: Repot each year, in midsummer.

Problems: Subject to rot if water accumulates in the top of the corm. Somewhat susceptible to both mealybugs and scale.

Erica
Heath, heather

The heaths are a large group of plants grown outdoors in cool northern landscapes. A few cultivars are commercially grown for cut flowers. Many of the smaller types, such as *E. gracilis* and *E. hyemalis,* make fine indoor plants if given enough light and cool temperatures the year around. The blooms are of varying colors and are usually quite fragrant. The plants are bushy and produce dense branches and tiny, narrow leaves that can be easily pruned or clipped. Heaths are very sensitive to soluble salts from excessive fertilizer or improper watering.

Light: Provide at least 4 hours of curtain-filtered sunlight from a bright south, east, or west window.

Water: Let plant approach dryness before watering, then water thoroughly and discard drainage.

Humidity: Requires moist air. Use a humidifier for best results.

Temperatures: 50° to 55° F at night, 60° to 65° F during the day.

Fertilization: Fertilize lightly once a year, in early spring.

Propagation: Take cuttings from stems or shoots that have recently matured.

Grooming: Keep to the desired height and shape with light pruning or clipping at any time.

Repotting: Repot in winter or early spring, as needed. A peat-based mix is essential.

Problems: Will not bloom if light is too low. Dry soil or a high level of soluble salts may damage roots, causing plant to die back.

Eucharis grandiflora
Amazon lily

Amazon lilies are easy-to-grow bulbs that will flower even in indirect light indoors. They are large plants with a wonderful fragrance. The flowers are white and borne in groups of 3 to 6 on a 2-foot stalk. The bulb may bloom as many as three times a year. Keep the plant very moist and well fertilized while it is growing. Only a short resting period is needed. Never let it get excessively dry, and keep the plant warm, especially at night.

Light: Place in a bright, indirectly lit south, east, or west window.

Water: Keep very moist during growth and flowering; at other times, allow to dry between waterings.

Humidity: Requires moist air. Use a humidifier for best results.

Temperatures: 65° to 70° F at night, 75° to 80° F during the day.

Fertilization: Fertilize only when plant is growing actively or flowering.

Propagation: Start new plants from the bulblets that develop beside the parent bulb.

Grooming: Give plant plenty of room to grow.

Repotting: Repot infrequently.

Problems: If plant is in a draft or dry air, leaves will scorch. Poor drainage, too-frequent watering, or standing in water will cause root rot.

Euphorbia pulcherrima
Poinsettia

The poinsettia was first found in Mexico in the 1800s, growing as a wildflower. It has since become the most popular living Christmas gift in the United States. The large, white, pink, red, yellow, lime green, or bicolor flowers are actually groups of bracts that surround a small, inconspicuous true flower. Ranging in height from 1 to 3 feet, the plants produce blossoms that are 6 to 12 inches wide.

With proper care these plants will continue to bloom for several months, and some can be made to blossom the following season. While blooming, the plants simply need plenty of sunlight and protection from drafts and sudden changes in temperature. Reduce water during the rest period from spring to midsummer, then increase waterings and apply fertilizer every 2 weeks. These plants normally flower in the fall, when the nights are long. Beginning about October 1, they need 2 weeks of long (14-hour) nights, uninterrupted by any light, before flowers are initiated. If your plant is indoors, be sure that household lights do not interrupt this darkness. You may have to place the plant in a dark closet at night or put it outdoors in a protected spot.

Light: Place in a bright, indirectly lit south, east, or west window.

Water: Keep evenly moist. Water thoroughly and discard drainage.

Humidity: Average indoor humidity levels.

Erica

Eucharis grandiflora

Euphorbia pulcherrima

Exacum affine

Felicia amelloides 'San Luis'

Freesia × *hybrida*

Temperatures: 50° to 55° F at night, 65° to 70° F during the day.
Fertilization: Fertilize when actively growing.
Propagation: Take cuttings from stems or shoots before they have hardened or matured.
Grooming: Prune after flowering. Pinch back stem tips of young or regrowing plants to improve form. Be careful not to remove flower buds when pruning.
Repotting: Repot infrequently in winter or early spring when needed.
Problems: If soil is too wet or too dry, or if plant is suddenly moved to a spot where light is low, leaves will drop. Poor drainage, overwatering, or standing in water will cause root rot.

Exacum affine
Persian violet

Persian violets are popular because they will bloom in small pots. Plants are commonly covered with tiny, blue or white flowers with yellow centers. Many florist shops carry them throughout the fall and winter in a variety of sizes from seedlings to blooming plants. The seedlings must be handled carefully, because slight injuries may lead to stem rot and cankering. Keep the seedlings in moist air and out of direct sun. As the plants get bigger, provide some direct sun in fall to encourage blooming. Never place the plants in cool drafts or water them with cold water.
Light: Keep in about 4 hours of direct sunlight in winter. Provide curtain-filtered sunlight in summer, from a south or west window.
Water: Keep evenly moist. Water thoroughly and discard drainage.
Humidity: Requires moist air. Use a humidifier for best results.
Temperatures: 55° to 60° F at night, 70° to 75° F during the day.
Fertilization: Fertilize only during late spring and summer.
Propagation: Start from seeds in spring. Sow in a small pot and transplant seedlings as needed. Or take stem cuttings, but cuttings do not produce as fine a plant as one grown from seed.
Grooming: Discard after flowering.
Repotting: Transplant seedlings several times, as they grow.

Problems: Dry soil or a high level of soluble salts may damage roots, causing plant to die back. Subject to crown rot in overly moist conditions. Susceptible to whiteflies.

Felicia amelloides
Felicia, blue marguerite, blue daisy

If they get an abundance of light, felicias produce their blue, yellow-centered blooms almost continuously. The plant is normally a little leggy and will need frequent clipping, but be careful not to clip off the stalks with flower buds. The leaves are ½-inch long, with a rough texture. Do not overfertilize this plant in winter.
Light: Provide 4 hours or more of direct sunlight from a south window.
Water: Let plant approach dryness before watering, then water thoroughly and discard drainage.
Humidity: Average indoor humidity levels.
Temperatures: 50° to 55° F at night, 65° to 70° F during the day.
Fertilization: Fertilize all year, more heavily in summer. Do not overfertilize in winter.
Propagation: Start from seeds in midsummer. Sow in a small pot and transplant seedlings as needed. Or take cuttings in spring.
Grooming: Keep to desired height and shape with light pruning or clipping at any time, being careful not to clip off the stalks with flower buds.
Repotting: Repot in winter or early spring, as needed.
Problems: Dry soil or a high level of soluble salts may damage roots, causing plant to die back. Will get spindly and weak if light is too low.

Freesia
Freesia

Freesias are bulbs grown widely in Europe and the United States for cut-flower arrangements. The flowers are extremely fragrant and come in many colors and patterns. You can force them into bloom as you would tulips or daffodils. Purchase mature bulbs in fall, pot them, and place the pot in a cool (not freezing) location until January. Then move the pot to a warm, brightly lit spot for forcing. Freesias can grow quite tall and may need staking. Unless you live in a mild-winter area, it is best to discard this plant after flowering. Freesias will not survive outdoors where it freezes in winter.

Light: Keep in about 4 hours of direct sunlight in winter while in bloom.

Water: Keep evenly moist. Water thoroughly and discard drainage.

Humidity: Average indoor humidity levels.

Temperatures: 50° to 55° F at night, 60° to 65° F during the day.

Fertilization: Do not fertilize.

Propagation: Buy mature bulbs or start new plants from the bulblets that develop beside the parent bulb.

Grooming: Generally discarded after blooming. In mild climates, bulbs may be planted outdoors.

Repotting: Not needed.

Problems: No significant problems.

Fuchsia × hybrida
Fuchsia, lady's-eardrops

The showy flowers and thin, green or variegated leaves of fuchsia make it a striking shrub. The sepals, which enclose the flower buds, are green on most plants; however, fuchsias have colored sepals that flare open to reveal pendant petals. The petals can be the same color as the sepals or a different hue. Colors range from white through pink, red, lavender, violet, and purple, in countless combinations. There are thousands of fuchsia strains, in a great number of shapes and sizes. Many make excellent hanging plants.

During summer, fuchsias can be moved outdoors to a cool-shaded spot. Feed frequently and always keep the soil moist. Plants in hanging baskets dry out quickly, so check them frequently.

Light: Keep in about 4 hours of direct sunlight in winter. Provide curtain-filtered sunlight in summer, from a south or west window.

Water: Keep very moist at all times, but do not allow to stand in water.

Humidity: Average indoor humidity levels.

Temperatures: 50° to 55° F at night, 60° to 65° F during the day.

Fertilization: Fertilize only during late spring and summer.

Propagation: Take cuttings from stems or shoots before they have hardened or matured.

Grooming: Prune in early spring. Pinch back stem tips of young or regrowing plants to improve form. Be careful not to remove flower buds when pruning.

Repotting: Repot each year.

Problems: Summer heat may cause plant to die back. If soil is too wet or too dry, leaves will drop. Susceptible to whiteflies. Check carefully for insects before bringing back indoors at the end of the summer.

Gardenia jasminoides
Gardenia, cape jasmine

Discovered in China in the 1700s, gardenia species now number about 200. The heady aroma of the creamy, spiraling blossoms is sure to please everyone. *G. jasminoides* has large, glossy, dark green leaves and produces an abundance of flowers. It is the type most often grown indoors. Some varieties bloom only in summer; others bloom throughout the year. Oil extracted from the flower is used in perfumes and tea. Gardenias also make excellent cut flowers.

These plants are popular additions to the greenhouse, and rightly so. Gardenias kept indoors need high humidity and cool nights as well as plenty of sunlight. The plant will not set flower buds if night temperatures exceed 65° F.

Light: Keep in about 4 hours of direct sunlight in winter. In summer, provide curtain-filtered sunlight from a south or west window.

Water: Keep very moist at all times, but do not allow to stand in water.

Humidity: Requires moist air. Use a humidifier for best results.

Temperatures: 50° to 55° F at night, 65° to 70° F during the day.

Fertilization: Use an acid-based fertilizer, and add trace elements once in spring.

Propagation: Take cuttings from stems or shoots that have recently matured.

Grooming: Prune in early spring. Pinch back stem tips of young or regrowing plants to improve form. Be careful not to remove flower buds when pruning.

Repotting: Repot infrequently.

Problems: Bud drop results from plant stress, caused by overly dry air, high temperatures, or a sudden change in environment. Plants purchased in bud, for example, will often lose all their flowers due to stress. If soil is too wet or too dry, leaves will drop. Will not bloom if light is too low.

Fuchsia × hybrida

Gardenia jasminoides

Gesneriad: *Aeschynanthus* 'Flash'

Gesneriad: *Achimenes* 'Menuette'

Gesneriads

African violets are the gesneriads most familiar to indoor gardeners. Once considered rather temperamental, they have been much improved in recent years. Many other, lesser-known gesneriads, such as nematanthus, gloxinias, and streptocarpus, are also available in florist shops, garden centers, and supermarkets.

The variety of forms and colorings of the more than 120 genera and 2,000 species in this family is truly outstanding. Gesneriads are classified according to rooting type and growth habit. African violets and episcias are two of the best known of the fibrous-rooted type. Tuberous-rooted gesneriads include florist's gloxinias (*Sinningia speciosa*). Achimenes is an example of the gesneriads that form scaly rhizomes underground. Most genera hybridize and cross easily within species, which leads to the development of many varied cultivars. Dwarf cultivars are now being developed, furthering both the usefulness of gesneriads and their popularity. Most gesneriads are easy to propagate, when plant patents permit. They serve well as children's plant projects or as gifts for plant-collecting friends.

Gesneriads are usually grown for their blossoms. Many, such as the episcias and columneas, have equally attractive foliage. Some get quite large and are useful as specimen plants to dominate arrangements in hanging baskets, or as pedestal plants. Many indoor gardeners grow gesneriads in a place with ideal conditions, then move them temporarily to display areas. Maintaining symmetry in the rosettes of foliage is the key to a specimen-quality gesneriad. Grow them on an evenly lit light bench for best results.

Since gesneriads have such variety, the following plant descriptions each include a care guide. In general, gesneriads adapt well to indoor culture. Most bloom for long periods, given good light. Many will adapt to lighted indoor gardens, plant shelves, or terrariums. They need warmth, even moisture, light fertilization, and no direct sunlight. The tuberous-rooted gesneriads and some of the rhizomatous kinds require a rest period after flowering, during which water and fertilizer should be reduced or completely withheld for a few weeks.

Achimenes
Achimenes, rainbow-flower, magic-flower, widow's-tear

Achimenes cultivars offer a variety of flower colors, including light blue, deep red, and yellow. They are often found in florist shops. Like their African violet relatives, they need warmth to grow well and ample light to blossom. Achimenes are bushy plants that are often used in hanging baskets. The foliage of many cultivars is attractive by itself, especially if the branches are properly pinched and trained when the plants are young. Achimenes are usually started from dormant rhizomes in spring. They will flower throughout the summer.

Light: Provide at least 4 hours of curtain-filtered sunlight from a bright south, east, or west window.

Water: Keep evenly moist. Water thoroughly and discard drainage. Do not water during dormant period.

Humidity: Requires moist air. Use a humidifier for best results.

Temperatures: 65° to 70° F at night, 75° to 80° F during the day.

Fertilization: Fertilize lightly each month while plant is growing actively.

Propagation: Start new plants by dividing and potting up rhizomes at the end of the dormant season. Or sow seeds in spring.

Grooming: Pinch back stem tips of young or regrowing plants to improve form, being careful not to remove flower buds.

Repotting: When plant has died back after flowering, remove rhizomes and repot. Store the rhizomes at 60° F, packing them in dry peat moss or vermiculite. Repot in spring. Keep recently potted plants warm and only moderately moist.

Problems: Will not bloom if light is too low. If soil is too wet or too dry, leaves will drop. Dry soil or a high level of soluble salts may damage roots, causing plant to die back.

Aeschynanthus
Basket vine, lipstick-plant

Basket vine is a hanging basket gesneriad that generally bears thick, waxy leaves on trailing or bushy stems. Depending on the variety, the tubular flowers are borne either at the leaf axils or in clusters at the ends of the stems.

They are usually brightly colored in shades of red, orange, pink, or yellow. The common name, lipstick-plant, comes from the fact that the base of the flower is encased in a tubular calyx, like lipstick extended from its tube.

Some varieties bloom strictly according to season, often in fall; others bloom intermittently throughout the year. The best-known species is *A. radicans* (sometimes found under the name *A. lobbianus*), a trailer with red blooms extending from a purplish calyx. *A. longicaulis* (formerly *A. marmoratus*) bears green and brown flowers that are not altogether attractive, but its purplish green, yellow-veined leaves have made it popular as a foliage plant. *A. hildebrandii* is a small, shrubby plant with numerous, bright orange flowers. Under good conditions, it may be everblooming.

These plants require night warmth and good winter light. They can be purchased from florists. Small plants will take some time before they will fill a large basket.

Light: Provide at least 4 hours of curtain-filtered sunlight from a south, east, or west window.
Water: Let dry slightly between waterings, then water thoroughly and discard drainage.
Humidity: Average indoor humidity levels.
Temperatures: 65° to 70° F at night, 75° to 80° F during the day.
Fertilization: Fertilize lightly each month from January through September.
Propagation: Take cuttings from stems or shoots before they have hardened or matured.
Grooming: Prune after flowering. Start new plants to replace old specimens when they get weak.
Repotting: Repot infrequently.
Problems: Will not bloom if light is too low. Dry soil or a high level of soluble salts may damage roots, causing plant to die back. Watch for mealybugs.

Alsobia
Alsobia, laceflower vine

Alsobias (formerly included in the genus *Episcia*) bear lightly hairy, dark green leaves, often with a reddish tinge in bright light, and form dense rosettes. From the rosettes, numerous creeping stems, or stolons, emerge, producing plantlets that root wherever they touch the potting mix. As the stolons arch downward, they form an attractive, thick covering of greenery, making alsobia an ideal hanging-basket plant. Heavily fringed, white flowers with various degrees of purple spotting appear intermittently throughout the year. Removing some of the stolons will increase flower production.

Light: Provide at least 4 hours of curtain-filtered sunlight from a bright south, east, or west window.
Water: Keep evenly moist when growing actively. Water thoroughly and discard drainage.
Humidity: Average indoor humidity levels.
Temperatures: 65° to 70° F at night, 75° to 80° F during the day.
Fertilization: Fertilize when the plant is growing actively or flowering.
Propagation: Remove and root plantlets, or propagate by layering.
Grooming: Remove yellowed leaves and faded flowers.
Repotting: Repot in late winter or spring as necessary.
Problems: Will not bloom if light is too low.

Chirita
Chirita

Chirita sinensis, the most popular chirita species, is known for its silver, marbled leaves and slow-growing, lavender flowers. It has a rosette growth pattern and is well suited to light benches or window boxes. It likes cool temperatures and is quite tolerant of dryness, being a near-succulent.

Light: Keep in about 4 hours of direct sunlight in winter. Provide curtain-filtered sunlight in summer, from a south or west window.
Water: Water thoroughly. Allow to dry out slightly between waterings.
Humidity: Average indoor humidity levels.
Temperatures: 55° to 60° F at night, 65° to 70° F during the day.
Fertilization: Fertilize regularly during the growing season.
Propagation: Take leaf cuttings at any time or propagate by division or from seed.

Gesneriad: *Alsobia dianthaflora*

Gesneriad: *Columnea sinensis*

Gesneriad: *Codonanthe digna*

Gesneriad: *Columnea* 'California Gold'
Gesneriad: *Episcia cupreata*

Grooming: Remove faded flowers and leaves promptly.
Repotting: Repot in spring, as needed.
Problems: Will not bloom in low light.

Codonanthe
Codonanthe

This gesneriad bears small, elliptic or rounded leaves on trailing stems, making it a good subject for hanging baskets. Flowers are small and white and, though not long lasting, are produced regularly throughout the year. If flowers are pollinated, colorful berries, often orange, white, or pink, will follow.
Light: Place in a bright, indirectly lit south, east, or west window.
Water: Keep thin-leaved varieties evenly moist at all times. Allow thicker-leaved varieties to dry slightly between waterings.
Humidity: Average indoor humidity levels.
Temperatures: 65° to 70° F at night, 75° to 80° F during the day.
Fertilization: Fertilize when plant is growing actively or flowering.
Propagation: Take stem cuttings anytime.
Grooming: Remove yellowed leaves and faded flowers. Prune excessively long stems.
Repotting: Repot infrequently.
Problems: Will not bloom if light is too low.

Columnea
Columnea

There are 150 different species of columnea. They come from Central America, South America, and the West Indies; their natural habitat is the damp tropical forest. Because they are semi-upright or trailing plants, they look especially fine in hanging baskets. The brightly colored, tubular flowers are orange, scarlet, or yellow, and many hybrids bloom continuously throughout the year. Flowers range in size from ½ to 4 inches, depending on the variety. Leaves vary from button size to 3 inches in length. *C.* × *banksii*, which has waxy leaves, is one of the easiest to grow. *C. gloriosa* has hairy leaves and red flowers. Two of the better-known hybrids are 'Early Bird' and 'Mary Ann'.

Columneas aren't the easiest plants to grow, but keeping the air moist will help them stay healthy and blooming. Water carefully during winter, and keep them away from heat sources.
Light: Provide at least 4 hours of curtain-filtered sunlight from a bright south, east, or west window.
Water: Keep moist during growth and flowering; at other times, allow to dry between waterings.
Humidity: Requires moist air. Use a humidifier for best results.
Temperatures: 55° to 60° F at night, 70° to 75° F during the day. Some species require much cooler night temperatures in winter to bloom well.
Fertilization: Fertilize only when plant is actively growing or flowering.
Propagation: Take cuttings from stems or shoots that have recently matured.
Grooming: Prune after flowering or fruiting. Pinch back new stem tips to improve form. Be careful not to remove flower buds when pruning.
Repotting: Repot infrequently.
Problems: Subject to crown rot in overly moist conditions. Will not bloom if light is too low.

Episcia
Episcia, flame-violet

Episcias are available in many cultivars, each with distinctive foliage texture and variegated coloring. Many gardeners value them for their foliage alone. In the summer, they produce small flowers that are red, yellow, orange, pink, lavender, or white. The plants produce short-stemmed rosettes of large leaves and trailing stolons on which smaller leaves appear. Episcias are generally used in hanging baskets or as ground covers in well-lit terrariums and dish gardens.
Light: Place in a bright, indirectly lit south, east, or west window or, even better, under fluorescent lights.
Water: Keep evenly moist during growth and flowering; at other times, allow to dry between waterings.
Humidity: Requires moist air. Use a humidifier for best results.
Temperatures: 65° to 70° F at night, 75° to 80° F during the day.
Fertilization: Fertilize when plant is growing actively or flowering.
Propagation: Pot plantlets or rooted side shoots as they form. Alternatively, layer the stolons or take leaf cuttings.

Grooming: For large leaves and plentiful flowers, thin stolons occasionally. Remove faded flowers and leaves.
Repotting: Repot in winter or early spring, as needed.
Problems: If plant is in a draft or dry air, leaves will scorch. Poor drainage, too-frequent watering, or standing in water will cause root rot.

Gesneria
Gesneria

Small plants with shiny, dark green, spoon-shaped leaves, gesneria are popular as terrarium plants. Within the moist confines of a terrarium, they are everblooming, with yellow, orange, or red tubular flowers. They require a high humidity to do well in the open. Gesnerias produce seed prolifically, often reseeding themselves throughout their terrarium homes. They get off to a fast start, often blooming only 4 months after seed is sown, but thereafter are extremely slow growing.
Light: Place in a bright, indirectly lit south, east, or west window or, even better, under lights.
Water: Keep evenly moist at all times.
Humidity: Requires very moist air. Use a humidifying tray or grow in a terrarium.
Temperatures: 65° to 70° F at night, 75° to 80° F during the day.
Fertilization: Fertilize when plant is growing actively or flowering.
Propagation: Start from seed or take stem cuttings from mature plants.
Grooming: Remove yellowed leaves and faded flowers.
Repotting: Repot infrequently.
Problems: Will not bloom if light or humidity is too low. May wilt or die if allowed to dry out.

Kohleria
Kohleria

Kohlerias are one of the gesneriads with herbaceous stems and soft, hairy foliage, typical of many members of this large family. Their tubular flowers are usually purple, red, pink, or yellow with strikingly marbled throats. They produce rhizomes and are easy to grow, but tend to get leggy when subjected to poor light. They are most often used in hanging baskets. Winter-flowering cultivars are common, but they need plenty of

light. Kohlerias go dormant after flowering. They can be cut back during this period.
Light: Provide at least 4 hours of curtain-filtered sunlight from a bright south, east, or west window.
Water: Keep very moist during growth and flowering. Spray occasionally when dormant.
Humidity: Requires moist air. Use a humidifier for best results.
Temperatures: 50° to 55° F at night, 60° to 65° F during the day.
Fertilization: Fertilize only when plant is growing actively or flowering.
Propagation: Take stem cuttings at any season, or divide rhizomes.
Grooming: Prune after flowering.
Repotting: Repot after flowering.
Problems: Will get spindly if exposed to low light and too much warmth.

Miniature Sinningia

Miniature sinningias, sometimes still referred to by their old name, gloxineras, are currently particularly popular, especially with gardeners who appreciate their ability to flower throughout the year with little care. They originated from crosses between large sinningias and the microminiature sinningias *S. pusilla* and *S. concinna*. Miniature sinningias bear tubular flowers with flared tips on short-stemmed rosettes rarely over 8 inches in diameter and often less than 2 inches in diameter. They come in a wide variety of flower colors.

Older varieties tend to go into dormancy after blooming, but modern hybrids produce new shoots even before the previous ones have faded, thus providing blooms throughout the year. The small hybrids are ideal for well-lit terrariums.
Light: Provide at least 4 hours of curtain-filtered sunlight from a bright south, east, or west window; or, even better, place under fluorescent lights.
Water: Water thoroughly and discard drainage. If tubers enter dormancy, stop watering until new growth appears.
Humidity: Requires moist air. Use a humidifier for best results.
Temperatures: 65° to 70° F at night, 75° to 80° F during the day.
Propagation: Remove and root extra rosettes. Or sow seed; many bloom in less than 5 months from seed.

Gesneriad: *Kohleria* 'Flirt'

Gesneriad: Miniature sinningias (left to right): 'Coral Baby', 'Ruffled Wood Nymph', 'Lyndon Lyon'

Gesneriad: *Nematanthus* 'Black Gold'

Gesneriad: *Saintpaulia ionantha*

Grooming: Remove faded rosettes.
Repotting: Repot annually in early spring or as plant comes out of dormancy.
Problems: Will not bloom if light is too low. Leaves will scorch if plant is in a draft or dry air.

Nematanthus
Goldfish-plant

Goldfish-plant produces flowers along its trailing stems, primarily in late summer and fall. The flowers resemble goldfish, complete with tiny "mouths." The foliage is small and grows close to the stems, which can reach 2 feet long or longer. Keep the plant in a hanging basket, out of drafts and dry air.
Light: Provide at least 4 hours of curtain-filtered sunlight from a bright south, east, or west window.
Water: Keep evenly moist. Water thoroughly and discard drainage.
Humidity: Average indoor humidity levels.
Temperatures: 55° to 60° F at night, 70° to 75° F during the day.
Fertilization: Fertilize only when plant is growing actively or flowering.
Propagation: Take stem cuttings at any time.
Grooming: Prune in early spring. Pinch back stem tips of young or re-growing plants to improve form. Be careful not to remove flower buds when pruning.
Repotting: Repot infrequently, in winter or early spring when needed.
Problems: Will not bloom if light is too low. Dry soil or a high level of soluble salts may damage roots, causing plant to die back. Susceptible to spider mites, especially if plant is too dry.

Saintpaulia
African violet

Originally collected in Africa in the late nineteenth century, African violets are first in any list of favorite flowering plants. No other plant can match their ability to thrive and bloom indoors for months on end.

Rosettes of velvety leaves on short stems surround clusters of flowers in white or shades of pink, red, violet, purple, or blue. The compact size of an African violet makes it perfect for windowsills, small tabletop arrangements, and hanging displays.

There are thousands of named African violets from which to choose. Some favorite standards include 'Swifty Thriller', 'Half Moon Bay', 'Nob Hill', 'Something Special', and 'Granger's Wonderland'. Consult local experts or plant catalogs to find your favorite.

Despite their reputation for being temperamental, African violets generally are not difficult to grow. The fact that millions of indoor gardeners grow and collect them attests to their ease of flowering. Plenty of bright, indirect light is the key to constant bloom. Supplement with artificial light if the plant stops blooming, especially in winter when it receives less than 12 hours of bright light a day. Evenly moist soil, warm temperatures, high humidity, and monthly feedings are the other important factors for growth. The plants will flower best with only one crown.

Miniature African violet varieties have recently gained popularity. Potted in 2½-inch pots, they grow only 6 inches wide, making them useful additions to terrariums or miniature greenhouses. Semi-miniatures have somewhat smaller leaves and crowns than the standards, but their flowers are almost as large. One of the most reliable miniatures is 'Mickey Mouse'. Outstanding semi-miniatures include 'Precious Pink', 'Snuggles', and 'Magic Blue'. Popular micro-miniatures include 'Optimara Rose Quartz' and 'Optimara Blue Sapphire'. Many trailing miniatures and semi-miniatures are available; among the most popular are 'Falling Snow', 'Snowy Trail', and 'Pixie Blue'. These do well in hanging baskets no larger than 4 inches in diameter. Group two or three in one basket.

In addition to the care techniques for standard African violets, there is an especially valuable tip for the miniatures and semi-miniatures: Keep the soil always moist. This can be difficult, because there isn't much soil in the small pots and it dries out quickly. For this reason, many growers like to keep these plants in self-watering containers.
Light: Bright light. Direct sunlight in winter is fine, but summer sun may be too strong. During winter, supplement with artificial light so that the plant receives at least 14 hours of light a day.

Water: Keep evenly moist. Use only room-temperature water. Avoid wetting foliage; cold water will spot the leaves. Leach soil occasionally.

Humidity: Provide moist air by surrounding base of plant with moist peat moss or by placing plant on humidifying tray.

Temperatures: 60° to 65° F at night, 72° to 75° F during the day. Keep plants away from cold windows. Sudden changes in temperature are harmful.

Fertilization: Fertilize all year, more heavily in summer.

Propagation: In spring, take leaf cuttings or sow seeds.

Grooming: Remove all dead leaves and flowers promptly (stems included). Shape by removing side shoots.

Repotting: Plant does best when slightly pot bound. Use pot about half the width of the plant. Plant rooted leaf cuttings in 2½-inch pots.

Problems: Mushy, brown blooms and buds indicate botrytis blight. Pick off diseased parts, provide good air circulation, avoid high humidity, and use fertilizer with less nitrogen.

Yellow rings on leaf surface are caused by cold water touching foliage. Streaked, misshapen leaves with irregular yellow spots are infected by a virus. There is no cure, so discard plant. If a healthy plant suddenly wilts, it has crown rot, which results from an erratic watering routine and is fatal. Do not allow the soil to dry out between waterings. Maintain a constant level of soil moisture. Severe temperature changes may also cause crown rot.

Lack of flowers is most often caused by inadequate light. Supplement daylight with artificial light. Extremely dry or cold air may also inhibit flowering. And repotting or moving the plant to a new location can inhibit flowering for a long time.

Yellowing leaves result from dry air, too much sun, incorrect watering, or improper fertilization. Follow fertilizer directions closely. Brown, brittle leaves develop if soil is deficient in nutrients. Repot if soil is old; otherwise, fertilize regularly.

Slow growth and leaves curled downward indicate that the temperature is too low. Soft foliage and few flowers indicate that the temperature is too high. Brown-edged leaves and small flowers result from low humidity. Place plants in humidifying trays.

Gesneriad: *Saintpaulia* 'Wine Country'

Gesneriad: *Saintpaulia* 'Snowy Trail'

Gesneriad: *Saintpaulia* 'Snuggles'

Gesneriad: *Saintpaulia* 'Little Rose Quartz'

Gesneriad: *Sinningia cardinalis*

Gesneriad: *Sinningia speciosa*

Gesneriad: *Smithiantha* 'Carmel'

Sinningia cardinalis, S. canescens
Cardinal flower, Brazilian edelweiss

These plants—cousins of the popular florist's gloxinia—were classified as *Rechsteineria* until recently. They are taller than florist's gloxinias and have tubular, red flowers about 2 inches long. Given enough light, they will bloom during the winter holidays and on into spring and summer. Like most gesneriads, they should be kept warm and only lightly fertilized. They may go completely dormant for long periods.

Light: Keep in about 4 hours of direct sunlight in winter. Provide curtain-filtered sunlight in summer, from a south or west window.

Water: Let plant approach dryness before watering, then water thoroughly and discard drainage.

Humidity: Requires moist air. Use a humidifier for best results.

Temperatures: 65° to 70° F at night, 75° to 80° F during the day.

Fertilization: Fertilize only during late spring and summer.

Propagation: Sow seeds in a small pot and transplant seedlings as needed. Or take cuttings in spring.

Grooming: Remove faded growth when plant goes dormant.

Repotting: Transplant seedlings several times, as they grow.

Problems: Subject to crown rot in overly moist conditions. Will not bloom if light is too low. Dry soil or a high level of soluble salts may damage roots, causing plant to die back.

Sinningia speciosa
Florist's gloxinia

Florist's gloxinias, originally from Brazil, have large, velvety leaves encircling bell-shaped flowers with ruffled edges. The flowers are borne well above the foliage.

To grow well and last for many years, florist's gloxinias need humidity, full sun in winter, and shade in summer. Keep the soil moist but not too wet, and be sure to use tepid water. After blooming, the plant needs a dormant period. While they are growing, gloxinias need fertilizing every 2 weeks.

Light: Place in a bright, indirectly lit south, east, or west window.

Water: Keep evenly moist. Water thoroughly and discard drainage. After flowering, gradually withhold water until the stems and leaves die back, then put the plant in a cool, dark place for 2 to 4 months while the tuber rests. Water sparingly until new growth appears, then repot into fresh soil, move into light, and provide moisture.

Humidity: Average indoor humidity levels.

Temperatures: 55° to 60° F at night, 70° to 75° F during the day.

Fertilization: Fertilize only when plant is growing actively or flowering.

Propagation: Sow seeds in a small pot and transplant seedlings as needed. Or take leaf or stem cuttings.

Grooming: Pick off yellowed leaves.

Repotting: Repot after dormancy, when growth resumes.

Problems: Subject to crown rot in overly moist conditions. Will not bloom if light is too low. Flower buds blast (buds form, but fail to open) when air is too dry.

Smithiantha
Temple-bells

This gesneriad produces an attractive spike of bell-shaped flowers from fall through winter, depending on the cultivar. The flowers are about 2 inches long and red, orange, yellow, or white. The semiwoody stems bear large, velvety leaves. Temple-bells need warmth and constant moisture to bloom well. They require less light than many other gesneriads, however. Some cultivars are large plants and will need plenty of room. After the plants bloom, allow them to go dormant, remove the rhizomes, and divide and store them until it is time for repotting in late summer.

Light: Place in a bright, indirectly lit south, east, or west window.

Water: Keep very moist during growth and flowering; at other times, allow to dry between waterings.

Humidity: Requires moist air. Use a humidifier for best results.

Temperatures: 65° to 70° F at night, 75° to 80° F during the day.

Fertilization: Fertilize only when plant is growing actively or flowering.

Propagation: Divide rhizomes. Seeds are also available, but can be more difficult than division.

Grooming: Remove old leaves as plant goes dormant. Cut flower stalks if you wish. Give plenty of room.
Repotting: Repot each year in late summer.
Problems: Leaves will scorch if plant is in a draft or dry air. Subject to crown rot in overly moist conditions.

Streptocarpus
Cape primrose

These plants are relatives of the African violet and the florist's gloxinia and can be grown under similar conditions. There are two quite distinct groups of streptocarpus: the stemless *Streptocarpus streptocarpus,* and the stem-bearing *Streptocarpus streptocarpella.* In common terms, the plants of the first group are streptocarpuses and those of the second are streptocarpellas.

Streptocarpus

These are commonly known as the Cape primrose because they are native to the southern tip of Africa and because their straplike leaves resemble those of the English primrose. Arching flower stalks, each bearing from two to over a dozen blooms, are borne directly from the stemless, narrow leaves. The latter can be up to 12 inches long. Many colorful varieties in white, pink, red, violet, or blue are available, often with contrasting veins and a yellow throat. Certain varieties, such as the seed-grown Weismoor hybrids, bear flowers over 3 inches in diameter on large plants, but bloom for only a few months, usually during summer. Smaller-flowered varieties, such as the Nymph hybrids (1- to 2-inch flowers) or the Mount Olympus hybrids (1-inch flowers), are more prolific, blooming the year around on smaller, more compact plants.

Cape primroses prefer cooler winter temperatures than their cousin the African violet. If the leaves go limp yet the potting medium still seems moist, the plant is suffering from overwatering or excess heat. Keep the plant drier than usual and place it in a shady spot until it has recovered.
Light: Place in a bright, indirectly lit south, east, or west window. Full winter sunlight will stimulate off-season bloom in these plants.

Water: Keep moist during growth and flowering; at other times, allow to dry between waterings.
Humidity: Requires moist air. Use a humidifier for best results.
Temperatures: 55° to 60° F at night, 70° to 85° F during the day.
Fertilization: Fertilize when plant is growing actively or flowering.
Propagation: Easily reproduced by division, seeds, or leaf cuttings. Leaves cut into sections and laid on the surface of rooting medium will each produce several plants.
Grooming: Pick off yellowed leaves and trim back those with brown tips. Cut flower stalks back after last bloom has faded.
Repotting: Repot in late winter or spring as necessary.
Problems: Wilting may occur if kept too moist or too hot. Will not bloom at high temperatures or in low light.

Streptocarpella

The stems of the streptocarpella bear small, thick leaves and arch gracefully over the edges of the pot, making it perfect for hanging baskets. Flowers are small but extremely numerous, especially during the summer months. Colors range from pale lavender to blue to deep purple, often with a lighter throat. Thick-leaved, pale-flowered *Streptocarpus saxorum* is the best known of the streptocarpellas; it needs full sun and blooms only during summer. The more modern hybrid streptocarpellas, such as deep blue 'Good Hope', bloom throughout the year with only moderate light.
Light: Provide at least 4 hours of curtain-filtered sunlight from a bright south, east, or west window. Full winter sunlight will stimulate off-season growth. *Streptocarpus saxorum* needs full sun to bloom.
Water: Keep moist during growth and flowering; at other times, allow to dry between waterings.
Humidity: Requires moist air. Use a humidifier for best results.
Temperatures: 65° to 70° F at night, 75° to 80° F during the day.
Fertilization: Fertilize when plant is growing actively or flowering.
Propagation: Take stem cuttings, although can be propagated also by division, seeds, or leaf cuttings.

Gesneriad: *Streptocarpus*

Gesneriad: *Streptocarpella* 'Good Hope'

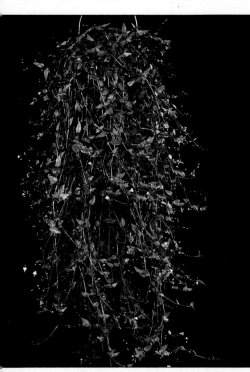

Gibasis geniculata

Gloriosa rothschildiana
Haemanthus katharinae

Grooming: Pick off yellowed leaves and trim back those with brown tips. Cut flower stalks back after last bloom has faded.

Repotting: Repot in late winter or spring as necessary.

Problems: Wilting may occur if kept too moist or too hot. Will not bloom at high temperatures or in low light.

Gibasis
Tahitian bridal-veil

This hanging-basket plant has small, pointed leaves—green above, purple below—borne oppositely along trailing stems. Given enough light, the plant will bear a profusion of tiny, delicate, white flowers on thin stalks above the foliage. This is where the name "bridal-veil" comes from. The plant is particularly sensitive to dry air and dry soil.

Light: Place in curtain-filtered sunlight to promote blooming, but no direct sunlight.

Water: Keep very moist at all times, but do not allow to stand in water.

Humidity: Requires moist air. Use a humidifier for best results.

Temperatures: 55° to 60° F at night, 70° to 75° F during the day.

Fertilization: Fertilize all year, more heavily in summer.

Propagation: Take stem cuttings.

Grooming: Pinch back stem tips of young or regrowing plants frequently to improve form, being careful not to remove flower buds. Start new plants to replace old specimens when they get leggy or weak.

Repotting: Repot in winter or early spring, as needed.

Problems: Will not bloom if light is too low. Dry soil or a high level of soluble salts may damage roots, causing plant to die back.

Gloriosa
Glory lily, climbing lily

Glory lily is a vining plant that has an extremely intricate, lily flower that grows to 4 inches across. The plant climbs vigorously and must be trained on a trellis. It will cling to the trellis with tendrils or "hooks" at the ends of its leaves. Glory lilies must be allowed moderate dormancy periods between growth cycles. The normal blooming period is midsummer through fall; however, it is possible, by varying the watering of the plant, to alter the resting-growing cycle and promote winter flowering. For winter flowering, the plant needs a well-lit location with good night warmth. *G. rothschildiana* has large, wavy-edged flowers that are brilliant red banded with yellow. *G. simplex* has orange-yellow flowers with slightly wavy edges. *G. superba* flowers are crimped along the edges, yellow aging to red.

Light: Keep in about 4 hours of direct sunlight in winter. Provide curtain-filtered sunlight in summer, from a south or a west window.

Water: Keep very moist during growth and flowering; at other times, allow to dry between waterings.

Humidity: Average indoor humidity levels.

Temperatures: 55° to 60° F at night, 70° to 75° F during the day.

Fertilization: Fertilize only when plant is growing actively or flowering.

Propagation: Start new plants from the bulblets that develop beside the parent bulb.

Grooming: Prune after flowering.

Repotting: Repot in winter or early spring, as needed.

Problems: Will not bloom if light is too low.

Haemanthus
Blood-lily

This bulbous plant is fairly easy to grow and will provide a splendid bloom to reward your efforts. The best-known species is *H. katharinae,* sometimes sold as *Scadoxus multiflorus subspecies katharinae,* whose feathery salmon flowers are borne in a globe-shaped flower head up to 9 inches across. *H. multiflorus* has a marbled flower stalk and bright red flowers in a cluster up to 6 inches across. Both bloom in early summer before or just after the foliage appears. The strap leaves, borne on a short stalk, remain on the plant throughout the summer, then fade as the plant enters winter dormancy. *H. albiflos* differs from the others not only in the flower—creamy white stems surrounded by a greenish white bract—but in that its stemless strap leaves do not die back in the winter.

Light: Provide at least 4 hours of curtain-filtered sunlight from a bright south, east, or west window.

Water: Keep evenly moist during growth and flowering; at other times, allow to dry between waterings.
Humidity: Requires moist air. Use a humidifier for best results.
Temperatures: 50° to 55° F at night, 65° to 70° F during the day.
Fertilization: Fertilize when plant is growing actively or flowering.
Propagation: *H. albiflos* produces bulblets, which can be removed and rooted. Others must be multiplied by seed, a long process beyond the skills of most home gardeners.
Grooming: Remove old leaves as plant goes dormant. Give plant plenty of room.
Repotting: Repot infrequently, since pot-bound plants bloom more profusely. Plant with the tip of the bulb protruding out of the soil.
Problems: Dry soil or a high level of soluble salts may damage roots, causing plant to die back.

Heliconia
Lobster-claw

Lobster-claw is a tropical New World plant grown for its exotic appearance. It bears smooth, often colorfully-veined leaves, like banana leaves, and striking and long-lasting inflorescences, either upright or arching downward, in combinations of yellow, orange, red, and green. The inflorescence is composed of triangular bracts in two ranks, which give the plant its common name. Most varieties available are dwarf selections, but even so they require large pots and plenty of space. They are often available as rhizome sections, which root easily.
Light: Place in a bright, indirectly lit south, east, or west window.
Water: Keep plant evenly moist at all times.
Humidity: Requires high humidity; grow on a humidity tray.
Temperatures: 65° to 70° F at night, 75° to 80° F during the day.
Fertilization: Fertilize when plant is growing actively or flowering.
Propagation: Divide rhizomes at any time.
Grooming: Remove yellowed leaves and faded flower bracts.
Repotting: Repot in spring as necessary.
Problems: Leaves scorch in low air humidity. Will not bloom in low light. Spider mites are a problem in dry air.

Heliotropium
Heliotrope

Heliotropes are semiwoody shrubs that can be grown as bushy plants (12 inches tall) or as single stems (3 to 4 feet tall). They are popular because of their extremely fragrant flowers, but they bloom only if given plenty of light. There are many hybrids available with purple, blue, or white flowers. The flowers are small and are borne in clusters 3 to 4 inches wide.
Light: Provide 4 hours or more of direct sunlight from a south window. Does best in a greenhouse setting.
Water: Keep evenly moist. Water thoroughly and discard drainage.
Humidity: Requires moist air. Use a humidifier for best results.
Temperatures: 50° to 55° F at night, 60° to 65° F during the day.
Fertilization: Fertilize all year, more heavily in summer.
Propagation: Take stem cuttings at any time. Or sow seeds, but seeds can be more difficult than cuttings.
Grooming: Prune after flowering.
Repotting: Transplant seedlings several times, as they grow. Repot in winter or early spring, as needed.
Problems: Will not bloom if light is too low. If soil is too wet or too dry, leaves will drop.

Helxine soleirolia

See *Soleirolia soleirolii*

Hibiscus rosa-sinensis
Hibiscus

A woody shrub, hibiscus is popular in outdoor landscapes in warm regions. Given plenty of light and kept pruned to about 3 feet, it is attractive and easy to grow indoors. The plants have large blooms, available in pink, red, yellow, orange, or white. Single and double flower forms are available. Individual hibiscus flowers are short-lived, but the plant blooms throughout the year. The plant is usually treated before purchase with a growth retardant to keep it dense and compact without any pruning. When the effect wears off, the plant will become more open and require pruning.

Heliconia latifolia

Heliotropium

Hibiscus rosa-sinensis 'Hula Girl'

Hippeastrum

Hoya carnosa 'Krinkle'

Light: Provide 4 hours or more of direct sunlight from a south window.
Water: Keep evenly moist. Water thoroughly and discard drainage.
Humidity: Requires moist air. Use a humidifier for best results.
Temperatures: 55° to 60° F at night, 70° to 75° F during the day.
Fertilization: Fertilize all year, more heavily in summer.
Propagation: Take cuttings from stems or shoots before they have hardened or matured.
Grooming: Keep to desired height and shape with light pruning or clipping at any time. Give plant plenty of room to grow.
Repotting: Repot in winter or early spring, as needed.
Problems: Susceptible to spider mites, especially if air is too dry. If plant is in a draft or dry air, leaves will scorch. Will not bloom in low light.

Hippeastrum
Amaryllis, Barbados lily

The strap leaves of the lilylike amaryllis emerge after it blooms. Its 1- to 2-foot stems have flower clusters that are 8 to 10 inches wide. They come in a wide array of colors: 'Apple Blossom' is pink, 'Beautiful Lady' is salmon-orange, 'Fire Dance' is bright red, and 'Scarlet Admiral' is deep scarlet. Seed-grown bulbs are sold by color in stores. Strains available through mail-order firms tend to produce more robust flowers.

The plant blooms in late winter and is moderately easy to grow; with proper care it lasts for many years. Pot bulbs in October. When a flower spike appears, place in a well-lit, cool (60° F) location. As buds grow and eventually flower, keep moist and fertilize monthly. After flowering, the foliage will grow for several months, then die back; allow the plant to dry out and become dormant.
Light: Place in a bright, indirectly lit south, east, or west window.
Water: Keep moist during growth and flowering; at other times, allow to dry between waterings.
Humidity: Average indoor humidity levels.
Temperatures: 50° to 55° F at night, 65° to 70° F during the day.
Fertilization: Fertilize only when plant is growing actively or flowering.

Propagation: Start any new plants from bulblets that develop beside the parent bulb.
Grooming: Pick off yellowed leaves.
Repotting: Repot every three to four years when bulb outgrows its pot.
Problems: Subject to crown rot in overly moist conditions.

Hoya
Hoya, waxplant

Hoyas are vining plants with thickened leaves produced on self-branching stems. Given enough light, they will produce clusters of extremely fragrant, waxy flowers in summer or fall, depending on the cultivar. The flowers form on the same spurs year after year, so be careful not to prune off these leafless vine extensions. Train the plants on a trellis or use them in a hanging basket. The vines will get quite long, but you can double them back to give the plant a denser appearance. Many forms have variegated or variously colored leaves. The most common plants are varieties of *H. carnosa*. *H. bella* is a small-leaved species that is also popular.
Light: Place in a bright, indirectly lit south, east, or west window.
Water: Keep very moist during growth and flowering; at other times, allow to dry between waterings.
Humidity: Average indoor humidity levels.
Temperatures: 50° to 55° F at night, 60° to 65° F during the day.
Fertilization: Fertilize only when plant is growing actively or flowering.
Propagation: Take stem cuttings at any time.
Grooming: Keep to desired height and shape with light pruning or clipping at any time, being careful not to cut off the flower spurs.
Repotting: Repot infrequently. New plants need to grow in a medium-to-large pot until almost root bound before they will bloom.
Problems: Will not bloom if light is too low.

Hyacinthus orientalis
Hyacinth

Hyacinths are usually purchased from florists for indoor blooms in late winter. Their fragrant blossoms are red, pink, blue, yellow, or white. During flowering they can be placed almost anywhere indoors, but need bright light to flourish. To force your own flowers, buy mature bulbs in October, pot them, and allow them to root in a cool, dark spot for 8 weeks. They should bloom 2 or 3 weeks after being brought into a warmer and brighter spot. Tend the plant until it dies back, then plant it in the garden.

Light: Provide at least 4 hours of curtain-filtered sunlight from a bright south, east, or west window after flowering has ceased.

Water: Keep very moist during growth and flowering; at other times, allow to dry between waterings.

Humidity: Average indoor humidity levels.

Temperatures: 50° to 55° F at night, 60° to 65° F during the day.

Fertilization: Do not fertilize when plant is blooming. Fertilize lightly at other times.

Propagation: Start new plants from the bulblets that develop beside the parent bulb.

Grooming: Remove old leaves as plant goes dormant. Cut flower stalks if you wish.

Repotting: Plant bulb in the garden after it goes dormant.

Problems: Poor drainage, too-frequent watering, or standing in water will cause root rot.

Hydrangea macrophylla
Hydrangea

Hydrangea flowers are 8 to 10 inches in diameter, immense clusters of ½- to 1-inch flowers. Shiny, oval leaves 2 to 6 inches long set off the flowers. The blooms are pink, red, white, blue, or mauve. Blue flowers will turn pink in neutral or alkaline soil. Adding aluminum sulfate or iron sulfate to the soil will produce blue flowers; applying lime or wood ashes will neutralize the soil pH and produce pink or red flowers.

The plant can be purchased in bloom during the spring or summer. It is easy to care for while flowering but will not usually bloom in the home the following season. For blooms to last 6 weeks, two conditions must be met: The plant must be in a cool location and the soil must never be allowed to dry. Daily watering may be necessary during flowering. If your tap water is especially hard, be sure to leach the soil frequently; use rainwater whenever possible. In mild

climates you can plant hydrangea outdoors for summer blooms.

Light: Provide at least 4 hours of curtain-filtered sunlight from a bright south, east, or west window.

Water: Keep very moist, but do not allow to stand in water.

Humidity: Average indoor humidity levels.

Temperatures: 50° to 55° F at night, 65° to 70° F during the day.

Fertilization: Fertilize when plant is growing actively or flowering.

Propagation: Take cuttings from stems or shoots that have recently matured.

Grooming: Discard after flowering, or prune and plant outdoors.

Repotting: Not usually done.

Problems: Dry soil or a high level of soluble salts may damage roots, causing plant to die back. If plant is in a draft or dry air, leaves will scorch.

Impatiens
Impatiens, balsam, patient-lucy, busy-lizzy

Growing impatiens is an easy way to bring natural color indoors all year. They're excellent decorations for a sunny table, window box, or windowsill. Regular care of impatiens will reward you with a constantly blossoming plant to brighten your home.

I. balsamina (common balsam) is an annual; it will bloom profusely for months in summer and winter, then die. Taller varieties of this species are usually grown in the garden. Although you may be tempted to bring outdoor plants indoors, their large size and lanky shape become more apparent and distracting once they are indoors. Dwarf varieties are far more attractive. Another species, *I. wallerana* (busy-lizzy), an everblooming perennial, is also easy to raise indoors. It is also known as *I. holstii* and *I. sultanii*. It grows up to 15 inches high, and has flowers 1 to 2 inches across in a wide array of colors—pink, red, orange, purple, white, and variegated. 'Tangerine' features a richly colored flower and handsome leaves.

The New Guinea hybrids (*I.* × *hawkeri*) were developed from a number of species native to New Guinea. These plants are perennials grown as annuals and are well suited to container culture. The flowers are large, and pink, red, orange, lavender, or purple. New Guinea

Hydrangea macrophylla

Impatiens wallerana 'Blitz'

Impatiens × *hawkeri* (New Guinea hybrid)

Ixora duffii

Jasmine: *Jasminum polyanthum*

hybrids need plenty of water and fertilizer and more light than other impatiens.
Light: Provide at least 4 hours of curtain-filtered sunlight from a bright south, east, or west window.
Water: Keep evenly moist. Water thoroughly and discard drainage.
Humidity: Average indoor humidity levels.
Temperatures: 50° to 55° F at night, 60° to 65° F during the day.
Fertilization: Fertilize all year, more heavily in summer.
Propagation: Start from seeds. Sow in a small pot and transplant seedlings as needed. Or grow from cuttings.
Grooming: Pinch back leggy branches to control shape and encourage blossoms.
Repotting: Transplant seedlings several times, as they grow. Plants that are slightly pot-bound will bloom more profusely.
Problems: Susceptible to spider mites, especially if air is too dry. If soil is too wet or too dry, leaves will drop. Will not bloom if light is too low. If you bring an impatiens in from the garden in fall, be sure it is free of pests, particularly whiteflies and spider mites.

Ixora

Ixora, flame-of-the-woods, jungle-geranium

Ixoras are compact, shrubby plants that bloom over an extended period beginning in summer. The stems bear large clusters of medium-sized flowers in red, yellow, orange, or white. The flower clusters tend to bend the stems, so you may wish to stake them during flowering. These plants need plenty of light and warmth to do well year after year.
Light: Provide 4 hours or more of direct sunlight from a south window. Does best in a greenhouse setting.
Water: Keep evenly moist. Water thoroughly and discard drainage.
Humidity: Requires moist air. Use a humidifier for best results.
Temperatures: 55° to 60° F at night, 70° to 75° F during the day.
Fertilization: Fertilize all year, more heavily in summer.
Propagation: Take cuttings from stems or shoots before they have hardened or matured.

Grooming: Prune after flowering.
Repotting: Repot in winter or early spring, as needed.
Problems: If light is too low, will get spindly and weak, and will not bloom.

Jasmines

Many types of plants are known under the name jasmine or jessamine. Those grown indoors generally have in common attractively perfumed flowers that are white to yellow in color and most highly scented at night. Most are twining and viny, requiring staking and regular pinching. The foliage is often shiny, making the plant attractive even when it is not in bloom. Their family background is varied: true jasmines (*Jasminum*) are in the Olive family; the others are in the Dogbane family, the Logania family, or the Nightshade family. Their flowering season also varies, but the most popular ones are winter or early spring bloomers.

Among the true jasmines, *J. polyanthum* is probably the most commonly grown. A winter bloomer, it bears dozens of scented, white, star-shaped flowers at a time, even as a small plant. Also popular is *J. grandiflorum* (poet's jasmine), bearing scented, white flowers in the summer. *J. sambac* 'Maid of Orleans' and *J. sambac* 'Grand Duke of Tuscany', known as Arabian jasmines, produce rose-shaped semidouble or double flowers that open a creamy white and fade to purple. Pungently scented, they bloom intermittently throughout the year. Arabian jasmines are more shrubby than most other jasmines.

Among the false jasmines, *Cestrum nocturnum* (night-blooming jasmine) bears greenish cream flowers from summer to fall. As the common name suggests, they are scented only at night. Both *Gelsemium sempervirens* (Carolina jessamine), which bears scented, yellow, trumpet-shaped blossoms, and *Trachelospermum jasminoides* (confederate-jasmine), with highly perfumed, white, star-shaped flowers, are hardier than the mostly subtropical true jasmines and can be grown outdoors in areas where temperatures do not drop far below zero. Indoors, both bloom in late winter or early spring.
Light: Provide 4 hours or more of direct sunlight from a south window. Does best in a greenhouse setting.

Water: Keep evenly moist during growth and flowering; at other times, allow to dry slightly between waterings.

Humidity: Average indoor humidity levels.

Temperatures: During summer, 65° to 70° F at night, 75° to 80° F during the day. During winter, lowering temperatures to 40° to 50° F at night will help stimulate flowering. Arabian jasmines prefer warmer winter night temperatures (60° to 65° F).

Fertilization: Fertilize all year, but more heavily during the growing season.

Propagation: Take stem cuttings at any time. *Gelsemium sempervirens* can be air-layered.

Grooming: Prune after flowering, removing overly long branches. Pinch back to improve form. Be careful not to pinch off flower buds. Can be trained up a trellis or other support.

Repotting: Repot at any time.

Problems: Will not bloom if light is too low. If soil is either too wet or too dry, leaves will drop. Spider mites are a problem when air is dry.

Justicia brandegeana
Shrimp-plant

The floral parts of the shrimp-plant, formerly classified as *Beloperone guttata*, are 3 to 4 inches long and hang downward. The tiny flowers are borne between scale-shaped bracts; together they resemble a shrimp. Cultivars are available in yellow, salmon, or red. The plants are woody shrubs that can grow quite large. Indoors, keep them pruned to about 2 feet.

Light: Keep in about 4 hours of direct sunlight in winter. Provide curtain-filtered sunlight in summer, from a south or west window.

Water: Let plant approach dryness before watering, then water thoroughly and discard drainage.

Humidity: Average indoor humidity levels.

Temperatures: 50° to 55° F at night, 65° to 70° F during the day.

Fertilization: Fertilize all year, more heavily in summer.

Propagation: Take stem cuttings at any time.

Grooming: Prune in early spring. Pinch back stem tips of young or regrowing plants to improve form. Be

Jasmine: *Gelsemium sempervirens*

Jasmine: *Trachelospermum jasminoides*

Justicia brandegeana

Justicia carnea

Lachenalia aloides

Lantana camara

careful not to remove flower buds when pruning.
Repotting: Repot at any time.
Problems: Will get spindly and weak if light is too low.

Justicia carnea
Kings-crown, Brazilian-plume

King's-crown is a large plant that bears groups of rose-colored flowers on spikes that grow above the foliage. It blooms in late summer. The leaves are 4 to 8 inches long, oval, and borne all along 2- to 3-foot stems. Keep the plant warm at all times; reduce fertilization after flowering.
Light: Keep in about 4 hours of direct sunlight in winter. Provide curtain-filtered sunlight in summer, from a south or west window.
Water: Keep evenly moist. Water thoroughly and discard drainage.
Humidity: Requires moist air. Use a humidifier for best results.
Temperatures: 55° to 60° F at night, 70° to 75° F during the day.
Fertilization: Fertilize all year, more heavily in summer.
Propagation: Take cuttings from stems or shoots before they have hardened or matured.
Grooming: Prune after flowering.
Repotting: Repot in winter or early spring, as needed.
Problems: If light is too low, will get spindly and weak, and will not bloom.

Lachenalia
Cape cowslip, leopard lily

Cape cowslips are becoming increasingly popular. They are bulbs and easy to force into bloom. Their striking multicolored yellow and red flowers add color and cheer to any household in winter. The leaves are large and sometimes have purple spots, adding interest to the plant. Most cultivars that bloom in late winter are planted in fall. As with any other bulb, the plant needs a dormancy period after the foliage has died back.
Light: Four hours or more of direct sunlight from a south window.
Water: Keep very moist during growth and flowering; at other times, allow to dry between waterings.
Humidity: Average indoor humidity levels.

Temperatures: 40°F to 45° F at night, 60° to 65° F during the day.
Fertilization: Fertilize only when plant is growing actively or flowering.
Propagation: Start new plants from the bulblets that develop beside the parent bulb.
Grooming: Remove old leaves as plant goes dormant.
Repotting: Repot infrequently.
Problems: Will not bloom if light is too low. Poor drainage, too-frequent watering, or standing in water will cause root rot.

Lantana
Lantana

Lantanas are small, woody shrubs that bear clusters of fragrant blossoms in red, yellow, white, and various bicolors. The flowers change color as they age, so a cluster usually will have a pleasing combination of light and dark flowers. The foliage has a distinctive aroma when crushed or bruised. The stems are prickly.

Indoors, lantanas bloom most profusely in early summer, but will bloom a little throughout the year if given plenty of light. The plants tend to get leggy if not clipped frequently. Lantanas are often used in hanging baskets; some cultivars are quite trailing in habit. If you are a devoted and patient gardener, you can train and prune lantanas into the shape of a tree. It would be best to do this in a greenhouse. Lantana, which can look and smell like lemon verbena, is quite poisonous.
Light: Provide 4 hours or more of direct sunlight from a south window. Does best in a greenhouse setting.
Water: Keep soil slightly moist at all times during the growing season, drier when the plant is resting.
Humidity: Requires moist air. Use a humidifier for best results.
Temperatures: 50° to 55° F at night, 65° to 70° F during the day.
Fertilization: Fertilize all year, more heavily in summer.
Propagation: Take stem cuttings at any time.
Grooming: Prune just before the heavy blossoming period. Keep to desired height and shape with light pruning or clipping at any time. Be careful not to cut off flower buds when pruning.

Repotting: Repot in winter or early spring, as needed.

Problems: If light is too low, will not bloom, and will get spindly and weak. If plant is in a draft or dry air, leaves will scorch. Whiteflies can be quite a nuisance; watch also for spider mites, aphids, and mealybugs.

Lilium longiflorum
Easter lily

Easter lilies are one of the most popular flowering potted plants sold in the United States. They are occasionally used as cut flowers. Blooming plants will last longer if they are kept cool, out of drafts, and constantly moist. To prolong the life of the flowers, remove the pollen-bearing, yellow anthers just as the flowers open. After flowering, care for the plant until the foliage yellows, placing it in a bright window and fertilizing it lightly. Most gardeners then plant the bulb outdoors in the garden, where it will flower every summer. You might get another Easter flowering if you leave the plant in its pot and move it outdoors, protect it from early freezes, and bring it indoors in late November. Force it to flower with high light and warmth.

Light: Will survive in low (reading-level) light. After flowering, place plant in a bright, indirectly lit south, east, or west window.

Water: Keep evenly moist. Water thoroughly and discard drainage.

Humidity: Average indoor humidity levels.

Temperatures: 50° to 55° F at night, 60° to 65° F during the day.

Fertilization: Do not fertilize when plant is in flower. Fertilize lightly at other times.

Propagation: Start new plants from the bulblets that develop beside the parent bulb.

Grooming: Remove faded flowers.

Repotting: Plant outdoors after foliage dies back.

Problems: Poor drainage, too-frequent watering, or standing in water will cause root rot.

Malpighia coccigera
Holly malpighia, miniature-holly

Malpighias are suitable for indoor gardens because they bloom as small plants, grow slowly, and seldom get more than a foot tall. Their leaves are similar to those of outdoor holly; though on the same plant some leaves are spiny and others not. The summer flowers are small and pink and are followed by red berries. Keep malpighias pruned into a shrub form.

Light: Provide at least 4 hours of curtain-filtered sunlight from a bright south, east, or west window.

Water: Let plant approach dryness before watering, then water thoroughly and discard drainage.

Humidity: Average indoor humidity levels.

Temperatures: 50° to 55° F at night, 65° to 70° F during the day.

Fertilization: Fertilize lightly throughout the growing season.

Propagation: Take cuttings from stems or shoots that have recently matured. Seeds are available, but can be more difficult than cuttings.

Grooming: Prune after flowering or fruiting.

Repotting: Repot infrequently.

Problems: Will not bloom if light is too low. Dry soil or a high level of soluble salts may damage roots, causing plant to die back.

Mandevilla sanderi
Dipladenia

Dipladenia is a woody-stemmed climber grown for its trumpet-shaped, five-petaled flowers. Up to 3 inches across, the flowers are light pink to deep rose with an orange to yellow throat. They appear from spring through autumn. The stems will twine around a support, or you can trim back the rampant growth to give the plant a shrubby appearance. Flowers appear on new growth, so heavy pruning will help stimulate new blooms.

Light: Place in a bright, indirectly lit south, east, or west window.

Water: Keep evenly moist during the growing season. During the winter rest period, allow to dry out between waterings.

Humidity: Average indoor humidity levels.

Lilium longiflorum var. *eximium*

Malpighia coccigera
Mandevilla 'Alice du Pont'

Mandevilla splendens

Mitriostigma axillare

Temperatures: 65° to 70° F at night, 75° to 80° F during the day. During the winter rest period, cooler temperatures (down to 50° F) are appreciated.

Fertilization: Fertilize when plant is growing actively or flowering.

Propagation: Not easy to propagate. Try taking stem cuttings, at any time, and rooting at warm temperatures using a rooting hormone.

Grooming: Remove yellowed leaves and faded flowers. Prune in fall to encourage plentiful new growth.

Repotting: Repot annually in spring.

Problems: Will not bloom if light is too low. Subject to spider mites and leaf drop in dry air.

Manettia cordifolia var. glabra
Firecracker vine

This plant is usually trained onto a small trellis. It is a little leggy for use in a hanging basket. Given good light, it will blossom throughout the year. The flowers are tubular, red, and tipped with yellow. They resemble a lighted firecracker.

Light: Provide at least 4 hours of curtain-filtered sunlight from a bright south, east, or west window.

Water: Keep evenly moist. Water thoroughly and discard drainage.

Humidity: Average indoor humidity levels.

Temperatures: 50° to 55° F at night, 65° to 70° F during the day.

Fertilization: Fertilize all year, more heavily in summer.

Propagation: Take stem cuttings at any time.

Grooming: Keep to desired height and shape with light pruning or clipping at any time.

Repotting: Repot in winter or early spring, as needed.

Problems: Will get spindly and weak if light is too low.

Medinilla magnifica
Medinilla

Medinilla magnifica is a well-chosen name for this plant, for it is indeed magnificent when in bloom. The drooping flower stalks, measuring up to 16 inches in length, are composed of pink bracts and clusters of bell-shaped, carmine flowers. The plant itself is quite striking, with woody, four-sided stems and large, leathery leaves with prominent veins. Prune it back harshly after each flowering to keep it at a reasonable size.

Light: Place in a bright, indirectly lit south, east, or west window.

Water: Keep evenly moist during the growing season. During the winter rest period, allow to dry out between waterings.

Humidity: Requires very high humidity. Place on a humidifying tray for best results.

Temperatures: 65° to 70° F at night, 75° to 80° F during the day.

Fertilization: Fertilize when plant is growing actively or flowering.

Propagation: Not easy to propagate. Try taking stem cuttings, at any time, and rooting at warm temperatures using a rooting hormone.

Grooming: Remove yellowed leaves and faded flowers. Prune after flowering.

Repotting: Repot annually in spring.

Problems: Will not bloom if light is too low. Subject to spider mites and leaf drop in dry air.

Mitriostigma axillare
African gardenia

This is a shrubby plant with deep green, ruffled, shiny leaves and small, trumpet-shaped, white flowers borne at the leaf axils. Its relationship to the gardenia is shown by the heady perfume the flowers give off. But it is far easier to grow indoors than a gardenia, adapting well to most indoor conditions.

Light: Place in a bright, indirectly lit south, east, or west window.

Water: Keep plant evenly moist at all times.

Humidity: Average indoor humidity levels.

Temperatures: 60° to 65° F at night, 70° to 75° F during the day.

Fertilization: Fertilize when the plant is growing actively or flowering.

Propagation: Take stem cuttings in spring.

Grooming: Prune to encourage plentiful new growth.

Repotting: Repot annually in spring for best growth.

Problems: Leaves may yellow if soil dries out or temperature is too low.

Murraya paniculata
Orange-jasmine

This tropical shrub, once restricted mainly to greenhouse use, is now finding a new life as a subject for indoor bonsai and topiary. It also makes an attractive indoor tree or shrub. It bears pale brown branches and glossy green, compound leaves. Its most attractive feature, however, is the small, perfumed, white flowers that combine the odors of jasmine and orange blossoms. It will bloom several times a year under good conditions. Well pruned, it can be kept to 3 feet high or less, but allowed to grow to its full height, it will reach an impressive 10 feet.

Light: Place in a bright, indirectly lit south, east, or west window.
Water: Keep evenly moist.
Humidity: Average indoor humidity levels.
Temperatures: 65° to 70° F at night, 75° to 80° F during the day. During the winter rest period, cooler temperatures (down to 50° F) are appreciated.
Fertilization: Fertilize when plant is growing actively or flowering.
Propagation: Take stem cuttings at any time.
Grooming: Remove yellowed leaves. Prune after flowering.
Repotting: Repot annually in spring for best growth.
Problems: Will not bloom if light is too low.

Muscari
Grape hyacinth

Small bulb plants, grape hyacinth are popular because they are easy to force into bloom. Their size makes them ideal windowsill or desk plants. The tiny, blue or white flowers are borne on 6-inch stalks in midwinter or early spring. They are fragrant and last for quite a while. The leaves are narrow and grassy, and arch outward from the bulb tip. Force them as you would other common bulbs: Purchase mature bulbs in October, pot and keep cool until January, then bring them into a warm room for flowering. Tend the plants until the foliage dies back, and then plant them in the garden.

Light: Place in a bright, indirectly lit south, east, or west window.

Water: Keep evenly moist. Water thoroughly and discard drainage.
Humidity: Average indoor humidity levels.
Temperatures: 40° to 45° F at night, 60° to 65° F during the day.
Fertilization: Do not fertilize when in flower. Fertilize lightly at other times of the year.
Propagation: Start new plants from the bulblets that develop beside the parent bulb.
Grooming: Pick off yellowed leaves.
Repotting: Transplant to outdoor location in spring.
Problems: No significant problems.

Narcissus
Daffodils, narcissus

There are two types of narcissus bulbs used indoors for forcing. The plants that produce a single, trumpet-shaped flower on a 12-inch stalk are called daffodils and are hardy bulbs. Those that produce a group of small flowers on a single stem are called Tazetta narcissus and are hardy only in the South. Many cultivars in either group are suitable for indoor gardens. Buy mature bulbs in the fall and put them in potting soil, pebbles, or sand so that half of the bulb sits above the water or planting medium. Keep them at 35° to 40° F for several weeks until they sprout about 4 inches of growth. Then bring them into a well-lit room for flowering. Keep them cool during this time and do not fertilize. Discard the plant after flowering, or if it is hardy, place it outdoors in a flower bed. Allow the leaves to die back naturally.

Light: Will survive in low (reading-level) light. After flowering, place in a bright window until foliage dies back.
Water: Keep very moist while flowering.
Humidity: Average indoor humidity levels.
Temperatures: 40° to 45° F at night, 60° to 65° F during the day.
Fertilization: Do not fertilize when plant is in flower. Fertilize lightly at other times.
Propagation: Buy mature bulbs or take a large division from the bulb of a garden plant.
Grooming: Discard or plant outdoors after flowering.
Repotting: Not necessary.
Problems: No special problems.

Muscari armeniacum

Narcissus poeticus

Nerium oleander

Orchid: *Brassavola perrinii*

Neomarica gracilis
Apostle-plant, walking-iris

The flattened, elongated leaves and general shape of the flower give the apostle-plant a resemblance to the iris. The plants are large, with blue and white flowers borne on tall stalks. Each stalk usually has one flower open at a time. It will last only for a day or two, but then another opens. It is a winter bloomer, so usually needs some direct winter sunlight. Plantlets will form at the tops of the flower stems. You can root them to start other blooming specimens.

Light: Keep in about 4 hours of direct sunlight in winter. Provide curtain-filtered sunlight in summer, from a south or west window.
Water: Keep evenly moist. Water thoroughly and discard drainage.
Humidity: Average indoor humidity levels.
Temperatures: 50° to 55° F at night, 65° to 70° F during the day.
Fertilization: Fertilize all year, more heavily in summer.
Propagation: Remove plantlets or rooted side shoots as they form.
Grooming: Cut flower stalks for better appearance if you wish.
Repotting: Repot infrequently. Pot-bound plants will bloom more abundantly.
Problems: Will not bloom if light is too low.

Nerium oleander
Oleander

Oleander is a popular indoor shrub, reaching over 6 feet tall under average home conditions. It bears narrow, glossy, willowlike leaves on upward-growing branches. Clusters of often highly scented, white, yellow, pink, or red flowers bloom in summer. Both single and double forms are available, and some varieties have the added attraction of variegated leaves. Oleander is often grown in tubs and placed outdoors for the summer. This stimulates heavier flowering. All parts of this plant are extremely poisonous, and it should not be grown where small children or pets have access to it. Always wash your hands after pruning and taking cuttings, to be sure you don't accidently ingest the sap.

Light: Keep in direct sunlight in winter. In summer provide 4 hours of bright, indirect sunlight from a south, east, or west window.
Water: Let the plant approach dryness before watering, then water thoroughly and discard drainage.
Humidity: Average indoor humidity levels.
Temperatures: 60° to 65° F at night, 70° to 75° F during the day. During the winter rest period, cooler temperatures (down to 50° F) are appreciated.
Fertilization: Fertilize when plant is growing actively.
Propagation: Take stem cuttings in early summer from branches not bearing flower buds.
Grooming: Prune severely after flowering. Pick up and destroy fallen leaves and faded flowers.
Repotting: Repot annually in spring for best growth.
Problems: Needs some direct sunlight to bloom. Watch for scale and spider mites.

Orchids

Growing exquisite orchids is regarded by most people as the supreme gardening achievement. But in fact, some species of orchids grow quite well indoors and require less routine care than other houseplants. In addition, improved breeding techniques have significantly increased the availability and lowered the cost of many cultivars. Placed on a windowsill in the living room, an orchid is sure to be the center of attention.

Orchids may have striking flowers, but their foliage is generally unattractive. They often have wrinkled, lumpy pseudobulbs at the base of the leaves and bear thick, aerial roots that many people find objectionable. Some indoor gardeners grow orchids among other houseplants, where their 'ugly duckling' appearance is not so noticeable, then move them to a more visible spot when they bloom.

It is wise to purchase mature, blooming orchids, as young plants can take years to flower. Described here are some of the orchids that grow well under average indoor conditions.

Aerides
Foxtail orchid

Aerides is a summer-flowering epiphyte of moderate size. Given full sun, this orchid blooms profusely, with fragrant flowers in red, pink, or white on long stalks that arch outward from the plant. *A. odorata* is particularly fragrant and popular with indoor orchid growers.

Angraecum
Comet orchid

Many angraecums are small plants well suited to indoor gardens. *A. superbum* 'Eburneum', which is larger than most, bears waxy, greenish white flowers and strap-shaped leaves. It, as do most angraecums, flowers in winter. The plants need brightness and even moisture, but are tolerant of cool night temperatures and normal household humidity.

Brassavola
Lady-of-the-night

Brassavolas are popular plants for beginners, since they bloom readily even under adverse conditions. The flowers are usually quite large for the size of the plant and greenish in color. Their most notable characteristic is that they are intensely fragrant, but only at night, which gives the group its common name. Best known are *B. nodosa* and *B. digbyana* (the latter is more properly classified as *Rhyncholaelia digbyana*). Brassavolas require abundant watering and full sun when in active growth.

Brassia
Spider orchid

Brassias bear flowers with long, narrow sepals that give rise to their common name. The plants are fairly large, with 15-inch flower spikes and leaves that grow to 10 inches long. They generally bloom in fall or winter if given sufficient sunlight.

Bulbophyllum

Bulbophyllums are the largest and most varied genus in the orchid family. Some are especially large plants with equally large flowers, but the most popular are dwarf or even miniature plants, which fit easily on even a narrow windowsill. Cultural requirements vary widely according to their native habitats, but most prefer warm temperatures, some shade from direct sun, and regular waterings while they are growing actively.

Cattleya

The genus *Cattleya* is not nearly as popular as the numerous hybrid genera derived from crosses between it and related orchids, such as *Rhyncholaelia, Laelia,* and *Sophronitis.* These breeder-made genera—among them × *Brassolaeliocattleya,* × *Laeliocattleya,* × *Sophrolaeliocattleya,* and × *Potinara*—are generally referred to by orchid fanciers as cattleyas or "catts." Cattleyas in the large sense include both the old-fashioned corsage orchids and an increasingly popular range of miniature hybrids with smaller blooms. The vigorous plants produce gorgeous blooms when they receive plenty of sun.

Cymbidium

The miniature cymbidiums are especially well suited for many indoor gardens. Yet even with miniatures, the narrow, arching foliage needs room. Give the plants cool nights to promote flowering, which usually occurs in late summer or fall. There are many hybrids available in a wide variety of colors. The flowers are long lasting, even in arrangements.

Dendrobium

Dendrobiums are mostly epiphytic orchids; both evergreen and deciduous types are available. Large flowers bloom in clusters or in a row along the stem. They last between a week and several months, depending on the species, and need plenty of sun, as do most orchids.

Epidendrum
Buttonhole orchid, clamshell orchid

Epidendrums are a large family of orchids, some growing as canes and others as pseudobulbs. Many species are small and suitable for warm, indoor window boxes in winter sun. Some species may bloom continuously under suitable conditions.

Orchid: *Cattleya*

Orchid: *Cymbidium*

Orchid: *Dendrobium*　Orchid: *Oncidium*

Orchid: *Cattleya*
Orchid: *Brassia*

Orchid: *Masdevallia veitchiana* 'Williams'

Orchid: *Miltonia*

Orchid: *Odontoglossum*

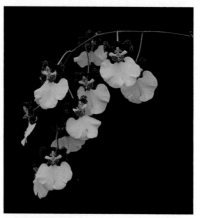

Orchid: *Oncidium*

Orchid: *Haemaria*

Haemaria discolor var. dawsoniana
Jewel orchid

The jewel orchid is one of several orchids grown as much for its exceptional foliage as for its bloom. This plant will grow in regular potting soil. It may reach a height of 8 inches or so on somewhat trailing stems. Its leaves are a velvety, purplish green, with a prominent network of red and white veins. Small, white or pinkish flowers grow on long spikes. When given good, indirect light, jewel orchids will bloom in winter.

Masdevallia
Tailed orchid

Masdevallias are cool-loving orchids that have curiously unorchidlike flowers: broad sepals partially joined at the base and pointed at the tips. They like bright light with little direct sun, and high humidity.

Miltonia
Pansy orchid

The flat-faced, heavily marbled flowers of pansy orchids give them their common name. The original genus has been subdivided into two closely related ones: *Miltonia* and *Miltoniopsis.* The former, which has two-leaved pseudobulbs, prefers warm temperatures the year around. *Miltoniopsis,* which has one-leaved pseudobulbs, prefers cooler temperatures. Both require filtered light and high air humidity.

Odontoglossum

Odontoglossums need moist air and stable growing conditions. They are best suited for greenhouses where they can get direct sunlight in winter and filtered light in summer. There are many species and hybrids available, most bearing large flowers that are fragrant and long lasting. Many bloom twice a year.

Oncidium
Dancing-lady

Oncidiums are a large group of epiphytic orchids. They generally produce stalks of yellow flowers speckled with brown. Flower size depends on the species, but is usually quite small. For the most part, they require bright light with protection from direct summer sunlight.

Paphiopedilum
Lady's-slipper

The long-lasting flowers of the paphiopedilum bear a distinctive pouch. Mostly terrestrial, paphiopedilums prefer a more humid, less airy growing medium than other orchids, which can be provided by adding extra sphagnum moss to their mix. There are two main groups: those with green leaves, which prefer cool growing conditions, and those with variegated leaves, which adapt well to regular indoor temperatures. All prefer filtered light.

Phalaenopsis
Moth-orchid

Moth-orchids are probably the best orchids for beginners. They adapt well to regular indoor temperatures (75° F during the day and 65° F at night), do not require excessively high air humidity, and are generally well suited to the average home. Unlike the many orchids that are grown solely for their flowers, moth-orchids often have attractively marbled foliage. They produce sprays of 2- to 3-inch flowers in a wide range of colors. Modern hybrids may bloom throughout much of the year. Close relatives requiring similar care include *Doritis* and the hybrid genus ✕ *Doritaenopsis.*

Rodriguezia

Most of the orchids in the *Rodriguezia* genus are miniatures, less than a foot tall. The plants bloom abundantly, producing large clusters of small, fragrant flowers, usually white or pinkish. Keep these plants moist and in damp air.

Vanda

Standard vandas are too large for most homes, but miniature hybrids are now available that are more suited to home culture. These plants prefer sunlight from a south window. They do well in greenhouses because of their need for strong light.

Care of Orchids

Orchids are an extremely varied group of plants, and their cultural requirements vary considerably, not only from one genus to another but from one species to another. This diversity makes it hard to give a general summary of orchid care, but it also means that there is an orchid that will adapt to just about every indoor situation. Always check on the cultural needs of an orchid before purchasing it; it is far easier to find an orchid that suits your conditions than to change your conditions to suit a particular species.

Light: Most orchids fall into one of two categories: those requiring direct sunlight and those preferring filtered light. The first group should be given full sun throughout the winter months, preferably in a south-facing window, and bright light with some shading from direct midday sun in summer. If they take on a yellowish tinge, all is well; if their foliage is bright green, they need more light. This group may need supplemental artificial light during the winter. The orchids that prefer filtered light are suited to either east or west windows or curtain-filtered summer windows the year around. They also do well under fluorescent lights.

Water: Varieties with thick leaves and large pseudobulbs prefer to be watered thoroughly, then allowed to dry out before the next watering. Those with thin roots and no pseudobulbs generally prefer being watered as soon as the potting mix starts to dry. Most orchids appreciate a short period of dry conditions in autumn to stimulate flowering.

Temperatures: Daytime temperatures of 70° to 75° F are generally acceptable throughout much of the year. A night temperature up to 15° F lower is appreciated. An annual period of cool temperatures (down to 50° F) combined with reduced watering will induce flowering in many orchids.

Fertilization: Fertilize lightly throughout the year, more heavily in summer.

Propagation: Most orchids can be divided every few years; at least three pseudobulbs should be left in each pot. Some also produce *keikis*, or plantlets, at the bases or on the flower stalks. These can be removed and potted up once they have produced roots.

Orchid: *Paphiopedilum*

Orchid: *Phalaenopsis*
Orchid: *Vanda*

Oxalis regnellii

Pachystachys lutea

Grooming: Pick off yellowed leaves and cut back flower stalks to the nearest green joint after blooming.

Repotting: Allow roots to extend beyond pot as long as plant continues to grow well. When growth is inhibited, repot into a larger container using an appropriate orchid potting mix. Very few orchids grow well in regular potting mixes, since they don't allow sufficient air circulation to the roots. Use a special orchid mix (generally a mixture of bark, perlite, sphagnum moss, and other bulky products). Many orchids will also grow on bark or on pieces of osmunda fiber. Tie them solidly to the support until they are well rooted.

Problems: Limp leaves or flowers are caused mainly by insufficient light, but can also be due to improper watering (usually overwatering). Yellowing leaves can be expected if leaves are old or plant is deciduous; otherwise, yellowing results from overwatering or sunburn. Brown spots are due to too much sun or to leaf spot disease.

Oxalis
Oxalis, peppermint stripe

Most oxalis are bulbous plants that rarely grow above 6 or 8 inches, although some with fibrous roots and upright stems do grow taller. Since they produce relatively large flowers (1 to 2 inches) all winter long, they make popular windowsill plants. Various cultivars are available in pink, white, or red. The foliage resembles clover, sometimes with a reddish hue. Cut off the flower stalks to prevent the messy petals and seed pods from dropping. Most bulbous types require a rest in the summer; they will die back as summer approaches. *O. braziliensis* produces wine red flowers in early spring over dense clumps of shiny, three-lobed leaves. *O. lobata* has yellow flowers held well above the foliage. *O. purpurea* (or *O. variabilis*) grows easily, with large, pink to rose red flowers. *O. regnellii* is one of the most distinctive and easiest to grow, with strong stalks of white flowers and precisely triangular leaf segments. *O. versicolor* (peppermint stripe) has an abundance of white flowers that are etched in red.

Light: Provide 4 hours or more of curtain-filtered light from a south window.

Water: Keep moist during growth and flowering; at other times, allow to dry between waterings.

Humidity: Average indoor humidity levels.

Temperatures: 50° to 55° F at night, 65° to 70° F during the day.

Fertilization: Fertilize only when plant is growing actively or flowering.

Propagation: Start new plants from the bulblets that develop beside the parent bulb. Grow fibrous-rooted oxalis from stem cuttings.

Grooming: Keep stemmed types to desired height and shape with light pruning or clipping at any time. Remove dead leaves and flowers from both types.

Repotting: Repot each year.

Problems: Susceptible to spider mites, especially if air is too dry. If plant is in a draft or dry air, leaves will scorch. Will get spindly and weak if light is too low.

Pachystachys lutea
Lollipop-plant

Lollipop-plant is a fast-growing shrub with decorative and long-lasting yellow bracts and short-lived but abundant white flowers. The leaves are large and puckered, slightly wavy along the edges. The bracts appear in conical clusters 4 to 6 inches long at the ends of the branches during the summer, or intermittently throughout the year under artificial light.

Light: Place in a bright, indirectly lit south, east, or west window. Grows well under artificial light.

Water: Keep evenly moist.

Humidity: Prefers high humidity. Keep plant on a humidifying tray during winter.

Temperatures: 65° to 70° F at night, 75° to 80° F during the day.

Fertilization: Fertilize when plant is growing actively or flowering.

Propagation: Take stem cuttings at any time; they root easily.

Grooming: Prune heavily after flowering to encourage plant to branch from the base. Most attractive when kept under 3 feet in height.

Repotting: Repot annually in spring for best growth.

Problems: Will not bloom if light is too low. Bottom leaf loss is normal, but can be reduced by heavy pruning.

Passiflora
Passionflower

Passionflowers are large, rapidly growing vines that cling with long tendrils to supports. The large flowers (4 to 6 inches wide) are complex and quite striking. *P. caerulea* has purple, white, and blue flowers in summer and autumn, followed by yellow, nonedible fruits. *P. coccinea* has showy, crimson flowers with protruding, bright yellow stamens. Its edible fruits are orange or yellow, striped with green. *P.* 'Incense' has fragrant, wavy, royal purple flowers in summer. *P. quadrangularis* is a standard fruiting passionflower with fragrant, white, pink, or violet flowers in summer. Because of its size, growth habit, and light requirements, this plant does best in a greenhouse or solarium. It should not require much care, except light pruning to keep it under control. However, it does need a dormancy period in late fall or early winter.

Light: Provide 4 hours or more of direct sunlight from a south window. Does best in a greenhouse setting.

Water: Keep moist during growth and flowering; at other times, allow to dry between waterings.

Humidity: Requires moist air. Use a humidifier for best results.

Temperatures: 55° to 60° F at night, 70° to 75° F during the day.

Fertilization: Fertilize only when plant is growing actively or flowering.

Propagation: Take stem cuttings at any time. Seeds are available, but can be more difficult than cuttings.

Grooming: Prune just before the heavy blossoming period, being careful not to remove flower buds.

Repotting: Repot infrequently.

Problems: Will not bloom if kept in low light.

Pelargonium
Florist's geranium, ivy geranium, Martha Washington geranium

Natives of South Africa, geraniums are versatile and appealing, available in thousands of species and named varieties. Some are grown outdoors; others can be easily moved indoors from outside. Common geraniums are hybrids of *P.* × *hortorum* and often have a dark green or blackish ring in each leaf. Varieties are available in red, salmon, apricot, tangerine, pink, and white.

Geraniums can add distinction to an indoor decor all year. They bloom in every season, but are most appreciated in January and February when little else is in flower. Many get quite large and need plenty of room, but there are also miniature and dwarf varieties of *P.* × *hortorum*. Fancy-leaf geraniums have varicolored leaves, often in bronzes, scarlets, and yellows.

P. × *domesticum* (Martha Washington or regal geranium) grows to about 2½ feet. It is most noteworthy for its flowers, which are large and come in a wide range of striking colors, some brilliantly blotched. Leaves are dark green, solid looking, with crinkled margins.

Scented-leaf varieties are grown primarily for the sharp, evocative fragrances of their leaves. *P. crispum* smells like lemon; *P. graveolens* and others, like rose; *P.* × *nervosum*, like lime; *P. odoratissimum*, like apple. They bear flowers that would be considered satisfactory in another genus but seem pale beside their larger cousins. In general the scented-leaf plants are smaller and less easygoing than the other geraniums. For example, they are more sensitive to over- or underwatering.

Ivy geraniums, varieties of *P. peltatum*, bear leathery leaves with a shape similar to English ivy and sport many clusters of showy flowers, often veined with a darker shade of the overall color. These are excellent in hanging baskets near windows.

Geraniums are easy to care for in the proper environment. A sunny windowsill where it is cool (never above 75° F) and dry is ideal. Fertilize once a week, and water when the soil is dry.

Light: Provide 4 hours or more of direct sunlight from a south window.

Water: Let plant approach dryness before watering, then water thoroughly and discard drainage.

Humidity: Average indoor humidity levels.

Temperatures: 55° to 60° F at night, 70° to 75° F during the day.

Fertilization: Fertilize all year, more heavily in summer.

Propagation: Take stem cuttings at any time. Seeds are also available for many cultivars.

Grooming: Pinch back stem tips of young or regrowing plants in autumn to improve form, being careful not to remove flower buds. Remove faded blossoms.

Passiflora caerulea

Pelargonium peltatum 'Galilee'

Plumbago auriculata

Pentas lanceolata

Primula malacoides

Repotting: Repot in winter or early spring, as needed. Transplant seedlings several times, as they grow.

Problems: If light is too low, plant will get spindly and weak, and will not bloom. Sometimes troubled by white-flies and by rots.

Pentas lanceolata
Pentas, Egyptian star-cluster

Pentas will bloom all year if given plenty of light. The small flowers, which are red, purple, pink, or white, are borne in clusters at the ends of the branches. Pinch and train the plant into a bushy form approximately 12 to 16 inches tall, but be careful not to cut off developing flower clusters. Stake the plant if flowers pull the shoots over.

Light: Provide 4 hours or more of direct sunlight from a south window.

Water: Keep evenly moist. Water thoroughly and discard drainage.

Humidity: Average indoor humidity levels.

Temperatures: 50° to 55° F at night, 65° to 70° F during the day.

Fertilization: Fertilize all year, more heavily in summer.

Propagation: Take stem cuttings at any time.

Grooming: Keep to desired height and shape with light pruning or clipping at any time.

Repotting: Repot in winter or early spring, as needed.

Problems: If plant is in a draft or dry air, leaves will scorch.

Plumbago indica
Plumbago, leadwort

Plumbago, a large-leaved semiwoody plant, tends to trail and is usually grown in a hanging basket or staked in a pot. It produces clusters of pale blue or white flowers. Plumbago grows slowly indoors and must be given ample light and warmth. For these reasons, it is best suited for greenhouses or solariums.

Light: Provide 4 hours or more of direct sunlight from a south window. Does best in a greenhouse setting.

Water: Keep evenly moist. Water thoroughly and discard drainage.

Humidity: Requires moist air. Use a humidifier for best results.

Temperatures: 65° to 70° F at night, 75° to 80° F during the day.

Fertilization: Fertilize all year, more heavily in summer.

Propagation: Take stem cuttings at any time. Seeds are available, but can be more difficult than cuttings.

Grooming: Keep to desired height and shape with light pruning or clipping at any time.

Repotting: Repot in winter or early spring, as needed.

Problems: If light is too low, will get spindly and weak, and will not bloom.

Primula
Primrose, Chinese primrose, fairy primrose, German primrose

Primroses produce magnificent clusters of flowers on stalks above a rosette of light green leaves in winter. Cultivars are available in red, yellow, blue, white, and bicolors. It takes plenty of light, moist air, and very cool nights to get these plants to flower properly. They are usually purchased already in bloom, although they can be started and grown in a home greenhouse, provided they are kept moist. Any stress will make them susceptible to spider mite infestation.

The three species especially suited to growing indoors are *P. malacoides*, *P. obconica*, and *P. sinensis*. The largest is *P. malacoides*, commonly called the fairy primrose. Star-shaped, scented flowers are borne in tiers on tall stalks. *P. obconica* (German primrose) reaches a foot in height and blooms in white, lilac, crimson, or salmon. *P. sinensis* (Chinese primrose) is the primula usually carried by florists. This small plant features delicate, ruffled flowers in a wide range of colors, pink being the most common. All these primroses need similar care.

A well-lit, cool area, such as a sun porch, is ideal. If the plant is near a warm, sunny window, pack coarse sphagnum moss up to the rim of the pot to help keep both the soil and the roots cool.

Light: Place in a bright, indirectly lit south, east, or west window while in flower. Before flowering, does best in a greenhouse setting.

Water: Keep evenly moist. Water thoroughly and discard drainage.

Humidity: Requires moist air. Use a humidifier for best results.

Temperatures: 40° to 45° F at night, 60° to 65° F during the day.

Fertilization: Do not fertilize when in flower. Fertilize lightly during the rest of the year.
Propagation: Start from seeds. Sow in a small pot and transplant seedlings as needed.
Grooming: Pick off yellowed leaves, and blossoms as they fade.
Repotting: Repot in winter or early spring, as needed.
Problems: Susceptible to spider mites, especially if air is too dry. If in a draft or dry air, leaves will scorch. Dry soil or a high level of soluble salts will damage roots, causing plant to die back.

Punica granatum 'Nana'
Dwarf pomegranate

Dwarf pomegranate, a form of the well-known tropical fruit tree, will do well in a greenhouse or solarium. The plant has small leaves similar to myrtle leaves. It produces showy red flowers, mainly in early summer. The 2-inch fruits are edible and will mature on the plant if kept warm and moist. Since the fruits tend to pull the branches over, the plant may require staking. Prune frequently to produce a woody shrub.
Light: Provide 4 hours or more of direct sunlight from a south window. Does best in a greenhouse setting.
Water: Keep evenly moist. Water thoroughly and discard drainage.
Humidity: Requires moist air. Use a humidifier for best results.
Temperatures: 55° to 60° F at night, 70° to 75° F during the day.
Fertilization: Fertilize only when plant is growing actively or flowering.
Propagation: Take cuttings from stems or shoots before they have hardened or matured.
Grooming: Keep to desired height and shape with light pruning or clipping at any time.
Repotting: Repot infrequently, in winter or early spring when needed.
Problems: Will not bloom if light is too low.

Rhododendron
Azalea, rhododendron

Many cultivars of azaleas and a few rhododendrons are available in bloom as houseplants. After flowering, many are simply used as indoor foliage plants. Some may survive if planted outdoors, although most azaleas sold as houseplants are not hardy enough for northern gardens. To encourage an azalea to bloom again inside the home, put the plant outside in early summer. Bring it back inside in early winter, after the cool days of fall, and put it in a cool place until it blooms again.
Light: May be placed anywhere when in bloom. After flowering, provide at least 4 hours of curtain-filtered sunlight from a bright south, east, or west window.
Water: Keep evenly moist. Water thoroughly and discard drainage.
Humidity: Requires moist air. Use a humidifier for best results.
Temperatures: 55° to 60° F at night, 70° to 75° F during the day.
Fertilization: Fertilize only when plant is growing actively or flowering. Use an acid-balanced fertilizer, and add trace elements once in spring.
Propagation: Take cuttings from stems or shoots before they have hardened or matured.
Grooming: Prune after flowering.
Repotting: Repot infrequently.
Problems: If plant is in a draft or dry air, leaves will scorch. Susceptible to spider mites, especially if air is too dry.

Rosa
Miniature rose

Although usually thought of as exquisite additions to outdoor gardens, miniature roses will also lend grace to your home. Delicate 1- to 1½-inch blooms are available in a wide range of colors. Grown as small bushes, climbers, or standards, they make an appealing indoor display. Their limited popularity stems from the difficulty gardeners have had in making them flourish indoors. However, new hybrids have eliminated many problems. 'Starina', 'Rainbow's End', 'Cupcake', 'Snow Bride', and 'Rise 'n' Shine' are a few reliable choices.

To grow miniatures successfully, give them the same care you would give them outdoors. Place them in a spot with abundant light and cool, well-circulated air. High humidity is a must, so place a humidifying tray beneath the pots. Allow the soil to dry slightly between thorough waterings. Apply a high-nitrogen fertilizer every 2 weeks. Rinse the leaves regularly with water, remove yellowing leaves, and clip off

Punica granatum 'Nana'

Rhododendron (Azalea)

Rosa 'Red Minimo' (Miniature)

Ruellia

Russelia equisetiformis

Scilla peruviana

the blossoms as soon as they fade. When pests, such as aphids or mites, invade, treat them immediately. After the last blossoms of summer have faded, prune back the plant severely.

Light: Keep in about 4 hours of direct sunlight in winter. Provide curtain-filtered sunlight in summer, from a south or west window.

Water: Keep evenly moist. Water thoroughly and discard drainage.

Humidity: Requires moist air. Use a humidifier for best results.

Temperatures: 50° to 55° F at night, 60° to 65° F during the day.

Fertilization: Fertilize all year, more heavily in summer.

Propagation: Take stem cuttings at any time.

Grooming: Keep to desired height and shape with light pruning or clipping at any time.

Repotting: Repot at any time.

Problems: Will not bloom if light is too low. If soil is too wet or too dry, leaves will drop. Susceptible to spider mites, especially if plant is too dry. Rinsing plant twice weekly sometimes prevents spider mites.

Ruellia
Monkey-plant, trailing velvetplant

The most commonly grown ruellia is *R. makoyana,* the monkey-plant. It blooms most heavily during fall and winter, producing rose red, trumpet-shaped flowers up to 2 inches in diameter. This plant remains attractive throughout the year because of its colorful leaves, which are silver-veined and velvety, olive green above and purple underneath. Another species, usually listed as *R. graecizans,* bears bright red, tubular flowers throughout the year over plain green foliage.

Light: Place in a bright, indirectly lit south, east, or west window.

Water: Keep evenly moist.

Humidity: Requires moist air. Use a humidifier for best results.

Temperatures: 65° to 70° F at night, 75° to 80° F during the day.

Fertilization: Fertilize when plant is growing actively or flowering.

Propagation: Take stem cuttings in spring or summer. *R. graecizans* can also be grown from seed.

Grooming: Pinch back regularly for full growth. Prune after flowering.

Repotting: Repot annually in spring for best growth.

Problems: Will not bloom if winter light is too low. Aphids can be a problem.

Russelia equisetiformis
Coralplant, fountain-plant

Russelias are hanging-basket plants that have arching branches of tiny leaves shaped like either needles or scales. The red flowers are borne on the ends of the branches, giving a cascading appearance. The plants are large, sometimes growing to 3 feet or more across. They must have plenty of light to continue blooming and to maintain a thick, vigorous branching habit.

Light: Provide 4 hours or more of direct sunlight from a south window. Does best in a greenhouse setting.

Water: Let plant approach dryness before watering, then water thoroughly and discard drainage.

Humidity: Requires moist air. Use a humidifier for best results.

Temperatures: 50° to 55° F at night, 65° to 70° F during the day.

Fertilization: Fertilize all year, more heavily in summer.

Propagation: Take cuttings from stems or shoots before they have hardened or matured.

Grooming: Start new plants to replace old specimens when they get weak. Give plant plenty of room.

Repotting: Transplant eventually to an 8-inch basket.

Problems: Poor drainage, too-frequent watering, or standing in water will cause root rot. Will not bloom if light is too low.

Scilla
Squill

Squill bulbs are commonly grown outdoors for their early spring flowers. The bell-shaped, blue flowers are produced on stalks 12 inches high. The moderate size of most squills makes them especially suited for winter flowering on a windowsill in the home. Plant several mature bulbs together in a pot in October and place in a cool, not freezing, spot until January. After they have flowered and the foliage has declined, you can plant them in the garden.

Light: Provide at least 4 hours of curtain-filtered sunlight from a bright south, east, or west window.
Water: Keep very moist during growth and flowering; at other times, allow to dry between waterings.
Humidity: Average indoor humidity levels.
Temperatures: 40° to 45° F at night, 60° to 65° F during the day.
Fertilization: Do not fertilize indoors.
Propagation: Start new plants from the bulblets that develop beside the parent bulb.
Grooming: Cut flower stalks if you wish. Remove old leaves as plant goes dormant. Plant outdoors when dormant.
Repotting: Not necessary.
Problems: No serious problems.

Senecio × hybridus
Cineraria

Cinerarias (also known by the name *Senecio cruentus*) are popular winter-blooming plants. Many florists stock them regularly. They can be grown easily from seed under cool conditions to produce a large cluster of flowers in colors from pink to dark blue. Some of the hybrid seedlings have dark foliage with a purplish cast when viewed from below. It is interesting to start with a seed mixture and see what different forms and flower colors you get. Give the plants plenty of light before flowering so that they will not become leggy. Keep them cool when blossoming.
Light: Provide at least 4 hours of curtain-filtered sunlight from a bright south, east, or west window.
Water: Keep evenly moist. Water thoroughly and discard drainage.
Humidity: Average indoor humidity levels.
Temperatures: 40° to 45° F at night, 60° to 65° F during the day, or cooler during flowering.
Fertilization: Do not fertilize when in flower. At other times, fertilize lightly.
Propagation: Start from seeds. Sow in a small pot and transplant seedlings as needed.
Grooming: Discard after flowering.
Repotting: Transplant seedlings several times, as they grow.
Problems: Subject to infestations of whiteflies, aphids, and spider mites. Powdery mildew is sometimes present.

Serissa foetida
Serissa, snow-rose

Bonsai enthusiasts can be credited with having introduced this attractive plant to indoor growers. Dwarf in all respects, serissa makes an attractive miniature tree or shrub, rarely reaching over 1 foot in height. It supports pruning well, allowing it to be trained into topiary or bonsai forms. The tiny leaves are elliptical and may be variegated in yellow. The flowers, borne most heavily in spring and summer, are barely ¼ inch in diameter and can be pink or white, single or double, depending on the clone. Although the epithet "*foetida*" means "foul smelling," the flowers themselves have no scent. The plant's disagreeable odor is noticeable only during root pruning. Plants with plain green leaves tend to flower more heavily than those with variegated leaves.
Light: Place in a bright, indirectly lit south, east, or west window.
Water: Keep evenly moist.
Humidity: Average indoor humidity levels.
Temperatures: 65° to 70° F at night, 70° to 75° F during the day.
Fertilization: Fertilize when plant is growing actively or flowering.
Propagation: Take stem cuttings in spring.
Grooming: Prune as needed.
Repotting: Repot annually in spring for best growth.
Problems: Will not bloom if light is too low. Spider mites a problem when air is too dry.

Solanum pseudocapsicum
Jerusalem cherry, Christmas-cherry

Jerusalem cherries are related to tomatoes, though the fruit is not edible. They need an abundance of light to bloom and set fruit properly. Many gardeners grow them outdoors and bring them in from September through the holidays. Given enough light, they will bear blossoms, green (immature) fruit, and orange or red (mature) fruit all at the same time. If you bring them in from outdoors, be sure they are free of pests, such as spider mites, whiteflies, and aphids. Pinch back the shoots on younger plants to keep their size to approximately 1 foot. If grown indoors the

Senecio × hybridus

Solanum pseudocapsicum

Spathiphyllum 'Mauna Loa'

Sprekelia formosissima

year around, the flowers should be hand-pollinated. Jerusalem cherries are usually treated as annuals and discarded after blooming, but they can be kept from year to year if trimmed back harshly.

Light: Provide 4 hours or more of direct sunlight from a south window. Does best in a greenhouse setting.
Water: Keep evenly moist. Water thoroughly and discard drainage.
Humidity: Requires moist air. Use a humidifier for best results.
Temperatures: 50° to 55° F at night, 60° to 65° F during the day.
Fertilization: Fertilize only when plant is growing actively or flowering.
Propagation: Start from seeds. Sow in a small pot and transplant as needed.
Grooming: Discard after flowering or fruiting. If treated as a perennial, prune harshly after flowering or fruiting. Pinch back stem tips of young or regrowing plants to improve form. Be careful not to remove flower buds when pruning. Discard when plant becomes too leggy.
Repotting: Repot in winter or early spring, as needed.
Problems: Foliage has an odor that some find objectionable. Susceptible to spider mites, whiteflies, and aphids.

Spathiphyllum
Peace-lily, spatheflower, snow flower, white anthurium

The distinctive flower of this plant gives it its common name, the peace-lily. The spathe is a pure white bract that encloses the true flowers. Sometimes more than 4 inches wide and 6 inches long, it unfurls to form a softly curved backdrop for the central column of tiny, closely set flowers. The blossom clearly resembles its relative anthurium. Spoon-shaped leaves on long stalks surround the flower and mirror its shape.

When not in flower, the peace-lily makes a particularly attractive foliage plant. Choose the plants by size: *S. 'Clevelandii'* (white anthurium) grows to a height of 2 feet. *S. floribundum* (snowflower) has leaves less than a foot tall. The most common, *S. 'Mauna Loa'*, reaches 3 feet. Other popular varieties include 'Sensation'®, the largest peace-lily, and 'Petite'. They bloom in spring and sometimes in autumn. A few days after it unfurls, the white spathe turns pale green.

Of the large flowering plants, this is one of the easiest to grow, especially under limited light conditions. A few hours of bright indirect light daily, normal to warm house temperatures, and regular watering and feeding are all that is needed to bring this plant to bloom.
Light: Will survive in low (reading-level) light.
Water: Keep very moist during growth and flowering; at other times, allow to dry between waterings.
Humidity: Average indoor humidity levels.
Temperatures: 55° to 60° F at night, 70° to 75° F during the day.
Fertilization: Fertilize only when plant is growing actively or flowering.
Propagation: Start new plants by dividing an old specimen.
Grooming: Pick off yellowed leaves.
Repotting: Repot infrequently.
Problems: Poor drainage, too-frequent watering, or standing in water will cause root rot. Will bloom poorly if light is too low. Cold drafts will harm plant. Wash leaves occasionally to protect plant from scales and mites.

Sprekelia formosissima
Aztec-lily, jacobean-lily, St. James lily

Aztec-lilies will last for several years in a pot if given ample light after blooming and allowed to rest in fall. The leaves of this medium-sized, bulbous plant are about 18 inches long and not particularly attractive, but they must be maintained to build the bulb for its next flowering. Keep the plant warm and well fertilized while growing.
Light: Provide 4 hours or more of direct sunlight from a south window.
Water: Keep moist when growing. When dormant, keep mostly dry, watering very occasionally.
Humidity: Average indoor humidity levels.
Temperatures: 60° to 65° F at night and 70° to 75° F during the day in the growing season (February through September); much cooler during fall and early winter.
Fertilization: Fertilize only when plant is growing actively or flowering.
Propagation: Start new plants from the bulblets that develop beside the parent bulb.
Grooming: Cut flower stalks if you wish. Remove old leaves as plant goes dormant.

Repotting: Repot every 3 or 4 years. Plant so that top of bulb is out of soil.
Problems: No serious problems.

Stephanotis floribunda
Stephanotis

Stephanotis is a vining plant that can grow quite large. It has thick, leathery leaves similar to those of waxplants. The flowers, which usually appear in June, are traditionally used in wedding bouquets. They are white and extremely fragrant. Given enough light, stephanotis will bloom most of the year. Allow the plant to rest during winter.
Light: Provide 4 hours or more of direct sunlight from a south window. Does best in a greenhouse setting.
Water: Keep very moist during growth and flowering; at other times, allow to dry between waterings.
Humidity: Average indoor humidity levels.
Temperatures: 55° to 60° F at night, 70° to 75° F during the day.
Fertilization: Fertilize only when plant is growing actively or flowering.
Propagation: Take stem cuttings at any time.
Grooming: Pinch back stem tips of young or regrowing plants to improve form. Prune after flowering. Be careful not to remove flower buds.
Repotting: Repot infrequently. New plants need to grow in a medium to large pot until almost root bound before they will bloom.
Problems: Susceptible to scale and mealybugs. Will not bloom if light is too low.

Strelitzia
Bird-of-paradise

Bird-of-paradise flowers are famous throughout the world for their beauty and form. They are large and are borne on a long stalk; many say they resemble the head of a tropical bird. The plant is also large, and will bloom only when mature. Bird-of-paradise is best suited for a greenhouse.
Light: Provide 4 hours or more of direct sunlight from a south window. Does best in a greenhouse setting.
Water: Water thoroughly, but allow to dry between waterings.
Humidity: Average indoor humidity levels.

Temperatures: 50° to 55° F at night, 65° to 70° F during the day.
Fertilization: Fertilize three times a year: spring, midsummer, and early fall.
Propagation: Start new plants by dividing an old specimen.
Grooming: Give plant plenty of room.
Repotting: New plants need to grow in a medium to large pot until almost root bound before they will bloom.
Problems: No serious problems.

Streptosolen jamesonii
Streptosolen

This is a winter-flowering, woody shrub; it produces clusters of bright orange flowers about 1 inch across. It tends to get leggy, so train it onto a small trellis or plant it in a hanging basket. Many gardeners prune it into a tree shape, with weeping or semitrailing growth at the top. Even in this form, it will need a trellis. Pruning regrowing stems will help maintain form but may limit blossoming. Though not common, it is occasionally available from specialty growers.
Light: Keep in about 4 hours of direct sunlight in winter. Provide curtain-filtered sunlight in summer, from a south or west window.
Water: Keep evenly moist. Water thoroughly and discard drainage.
Humidity: Average indoor humidity levels.
Temperatures: 50° to 55° F at night, 60° to 65° F during the day.
Fertilization: Fertilize all year, more heavily in summer.
Propagation: Take stem cuttings at any time.
Grooming: Prune in early spring. Pinch back stem tips of young or regrowing plants to improve form. Be careful not to destroy flower buds when pruning.
Repotting: Repot infrequently. New plants need to grow in a medium to large pot until almost root bound before they will bloom.
Problems: Will get spindly and weak if light is too low. If soil is too wet or too dry, leaves will drop.

Stephanotis floribunda

Strelitzia reginae

Streptosolen jamesonii

Tabernaemontana divaricata

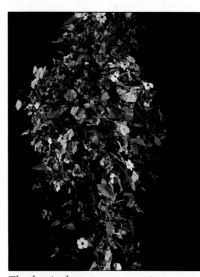

Thunbergia alata

Tulbaghia fragrans

Tabernaemontana divaricata
Butterfly-gardenia, crape-jasmine, Adam's-apple, Nero's-crown

Butterfly-gardenia (sometimes classified as *Ervatamia coronaria*) is a large shrub. It produces clusters of fragrant flowers that are about 2 inches across. Most of the flowers appear in summer, but good light will prolong the blooming period. *T. divaricata plena* is a species with double-petaled flowers. The plants will grow to about 2 feet and should be pruned into a neat shape. Although a slow grower, several years of good care should produce a specimen plant. Always water thoroughly to prevent a buildup of soluble salts, which will cause the plant to decline.

Light: Provide 4 hours or more of direct sunlight from a south window. Does best in a greenhouse setting.
Water: Keep very moist at all times, but do not allow to stand in water.
Humidity: Average indoor humidity levels.
Temperatures: 65° to 70° F at night, 75° to 80° F during the day.
Fertilization: Fertilize all year, more heavily in summer.
Propagation: Take cuttings from stems or shoots before they have hardened or matured.
Grooming: Prune in early spring.
Repotting: Repot infrequently.
Problems: Will not bloom if light is too low. Dry soil or a high level of soluble salts may damage roots, causing plant to die back.

Tetranema roseum
Mexican foxglove

Mexican foxglove bears groups of tiny, pink blossoms on 8-inch stalks, all year long. The dark green leaves of this small plant are formed in a rosette on a short stem. To keep it blooming, give it warmth, even moisture, and plenty of winter light. Keep Mexican foxglove out of cold drafts. Works well as a terrarium plant.

Light: Keep in about 4 hours of direct sunlight in winter. Provide curtain-filtered sunlight in summer, from a south or west window.
Water: Keep evenly moist. Water thoroughly and discard drainage.
Humidity: Average indoor humidity levels.

Temperatures: 55° to 60° F at night, 70° to 75° F during the day.
Fertilization: Fertilize all year, more heavily in summer.
Propagation: Grow from seed, which is generally available and easy to germinate, or start new plants by dividing an old specimen.
Grooming: Pick off yellowed leaves. Cut flower stalks if you wish.
Repotting: Repot at any time.
Problems: If plant is in a draft or dry air, leaves will scorch.

Thunbergia alata
Thunbergia, black-eyed-susan, clock vine

A spring-flowering plant popular with florists, thunbergia is generally used in a hanging basket for a patio garden. It can also be trained onto a small trellis. Its yellow flowers with black centers resemble the pastureweed common in northern states. In the South, thunbergia grows as a perennial vine. Indoor gardeners can keep it from year to year, but it needs plenty of light to flower well. The plants may get weak and spindly after a few years, even with the best care.

Light: Provide 4 hours or more of direct sunlight from a south window. Does best in a greenhouse setting.
Water: Keep evenly moist. Water thoroughly and discard drainage.
Humidity: Average indoor humidity levels.
Temperatures: 55° to 60° F at night, 70° to 75° F during the day.
Fertilization: Fertilize only when plant is growing actively or flowering.
Propagation: Start from seeds. Sow in a small pot and transplant seedlings as needed. Sow in early to midsummer for fall and winter flowers.
Grooming: Cut back straggly vines at the base. Trim the others lightly. Pinch off faded flowers to prolong flowering.
Repotting: Cut back and repot when flowering stops.
Problems: Will not bloom if light is too low.

Tulbaghia fragrans
Fragrant tulbaghia, society-garlic, violet tulbaghia

Although tulbaghias are bulbs, they bloom repeatedly throughout the year if given plenty of light, water, and fertilizer.

The flowers are borne in clusters on 15-inch stalks. They are usually lavender and mildly fragrant. Do not bruise or break the leaves unless you like the smell of garlic in your indoor garden. The bulbs multiply rapidly and require frequent division.
Light: Give 4 hours or more of direct sunlight from a south window.
Water: Keep evenly moist. Water thoroughly and discard drainage.
Humidity: Average indoor humidity levels.
Temperatures: 40° to 45° F at night, 60° to 65° F during the day.
Fertilization: Fertilize all year, more heavily in summer.
Propagation: Start new plants by dividing an old specimen.
Grooming: Pick off yellowed leaves.
Repotting: Repot each year.
Problems: Will not bloom if light is too low.

Tulipa
Tulip

There are hundreds of tulip varieties. Most are suitable for indoor forcing, though the smaller varieties may be the easiest to force successfully. Tulips can be purchased already in bud from many florists. To force your own, purchase several mature bulbs in October, put them together in a pot with the flat side outward to get better foliage orientation, and place them in a cool spot until January or February. Many devoted indoor gardeners use an old refrigerator to keep the bulbs cool. After the bulbs have flowered and the foliage has died back, most varieties can be placed in the garden. The bulbs of some varieties will divide readily; others are more difficult to propagate.
Light: Place anywhere during flowering. Before and after flowering, provide at least 4 hours of curtain-filtered sunlight from a bright south, east, or west window.
Water: Keep very moist during growth and flowering; at other times, allow to dry between waterings.
Humidity: Average indoor humidity levels.
Temperatures: 50° to 55° F at night, 60° to 65° F during the day.
Fertilization: Lightly fertilize after flowering.

Propagation: Start new plants from the bulblets that develop beside the parent bulb.
Grooming: Cut flower stalks if you wish. Remove old leaves.
Repotting: Repot each year.
Problems: Subject to crown rot in overly moist conditions.

Vallota
Scarborough-lily

This bulb produces up to 10 bright red-orange flowers in a cluster on a 2-foot stalk. It usually flowers in summer or early fall. The leaves are narrow and about a foot long. After they have died back, give the bulb a rest until summer. Repot it gently each summer, disturbing the roots in the center of the rootball as little as possible.
Light: Provide 4 hours or more of direct sunlight from a south window.
Water: Keep very moist during growth and flowering; at other times, allow to dry between waterings.
Humidity: Average indoor humidity levels.
Temperatures: 50° to 55° F at night, 60° to 65° F during the day.
Fertilization: Do not fertilize when flowering. Fertilize lightly at other times.
Propagation: Start new plants from the bulblets that develop beside the parent bulb.
Grooming: Cut flower stalks if you wish. Remove old leaves as plant goes dormant.
Repotting: Repot each year.
Problems: Subject to crown rot in overly moist conditions.

Veltheimia
Veltheimia, forest lily

Veltheimias are large bulbs. The tubular pink, rose, or white flowers are borne in winter and early spring on a stalk 12 to 15 inches high. The glossy green leaves are 12 inches long and arch outward from the base of the flower stalk. Give bulbs a rest in summer.
Light: Provide at least 4 hours of curtain-filtered sunlight from a bright south, east, or west window.
Water: Keep very moist during growth and flowering. Allow to dry out during the summer.
Humidity: Average indoor humidity levels.
Temperatures: 50° to 55° F at night, 60° to 65° F during the day.

Tulipa

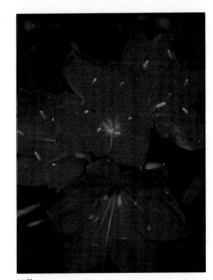

Vallota

Veltheimia

Zantedeschia aethiopica

Zephyranthes candida

Fertilization: Fertilize only when plant is growing actively or flowering.
Propagation: Start new plants from the bulblets that develop beside the parent bulb.
Grooming: Pick off yellowed leaves. Cut flower stalks if you wish.
Repotting: Repot when growth starts in fall.
Problems: No serious problems.

Zantedeschia
Calla lily, golden calla, pink calla

The elegant flower of the calla lily, actually a colored leaf, called a spathe, which curls around a fragrant, yellow column of flowers, needs no introduction. Most people recognize it on sight. Besides being a popular cut flower, calla lilies also make good houseplants.

The best-known calla lily is the largest: *Zantedeschia aethiopica*. It bears creamy white spathes, 5 to 10 inches in length, atop wide, glossy, arrow- or heart-shaped leaves. It can reach 4 feet or more in height when in flower, but some cultivars are much smaller. Other species include *Z. elliottiana* (golden calla), which has white-spotted, arrow-shaped leaves, and *Z. rehmannii* (pink calla) with strap-shaped leaves often covered with white dots. Hybrid callas in shades of white, pink, yellow, orange, and red, often dwarf plants no more than 18 inches in height, are becoming increasingly popular.

Callas are native to bogs that dry up completely during the dry season, which gives a clue as to their culture. Since their flowers are most appreciated during the winter months, begin watering lightly in fall, increasing the amount until the plant is in full growth. Alternatively, start them in spring for summer bloom. Keep the potting mix evenly moist during growth and flowering. *Z. aethiopica* especially likes moist soil; it will grow even with its pot sitting permanently in water. When blooms fade, reduce watering, removing the leaves as they yellow. If the plant goes entirely dormant, keep the rhizome nearly dry, watering it only enough to keep it from shriveling, until the following growing and flowering season. Some cultivars will maintain their foliage throughout the year, and these should be kept slightly moist at all times.

Light: Keep in 4 hours of direct sunlight in winter. Provide curtain-filtered sunlight in summer from a south or west window.
Water: Keep thoroughly moist during growth and flowering; at other times, allow to dry between waterings.
Humidity: Requires moist air. Use a humidifier for best results.
Temperatures: 50° to 55° F at night, 65° to 70° F during the day. During dormancy, temperature is not a major factor.
Fertilization: Fertilize only when plant is growing actively or flowering.
Propagation: Start new plants by dividing an old specimen.
Grooming: Pick off yellowed leaves. Cut faded flower stalks.
Repotting: Repot the rhizome at the end of dormancy.
Problems: If plant is in a draft or dry air, leaves will scorch. Spider mites can be a problem if air is too dry.

Zephyranthes
Zephyr-lily

Many species and hybrids of zephyr-lilies are available. Most are of moderate size and are easy to grow. They bloom at various times, sometimes more than once a year. Flowers are pink, yellow, orange, or white and are borne singly on a stalk, like a daffodil. The foliage is grassy and about a foot long. Give the plants a rest period of 2 months after the foliage has died back. Keep in a sunny, cool spot for flowering.

Light: Provide 4 hours or more of direct sunlight from a south window.
Water: Keep very moist during growth and flowering; at other times, allow to dry between waterings.
Humidity: Average indoor humidity levels.
Temperatures: 40° to 45° F at night, 60° to 65° F during the day.
Fertilization: Fertilize only when plant is growing actively or flowering.
Propagation: Start new plants from the bulblets that develop beside the parent bulb.
Grooming: Cut flower stalks if you wish. Remove old leaves as plant goes dormant.
Repotting: Repot each year.
Problems: Poor drainage, too-frequent watering, or standing in water will cause root rot.

Foliage Houseplants

A brief look at this section reveals the wide range of plants considered noteworthy for their foliage. Foliage attributes include color, variegation, and texture and also the size and arrangement of the leaves on the stems and branches. Even though striking and colorful foliage is important, the size, shape, and form of a plant are the major criteria for its selection as a decorative accent or part of an indoor garden. It is the combination of these characteristics—size, shape, form, and foliage—that gives an indoor garden its special charm. The ability to determine the relative importance of these characteristics enables interior plant designers to create striking indoor settings.

Many foliage plants produce flowers from time to time, but in general their flowers are less significant for design purposes than are their other characteristics. In some cases a plant may produce flowers only under precise cultural conditions, limiting its usefulness as a flowering specimen.

When selecting foliage plants, use the cultural information given here to find a plant that will fit both your design purposes and setting.

Acorus gramineus 'Variegatus'

Acorus gramineus
Miniature flagplant, Japanese sweet flag

Flagplants are often grown outdoors in southern climates, but two cultivars are suited for indoor gardening: a dwarf variety that has green leaves and a taller, variegated form. Their leaves look like stiff, thick blades of grass. The plants are easy to grow in a variety of indoor settings. They do best in bright light, moist soil, and high humidity. In locations with only moderate light, keep them drier and fertilize less. Flagplants do well in cool spots if not overwatered.
Light: Provide at least moderate light but no direct sunlight.
Water: Keep evenly moist. Water thoroughly and discard drainage.
Humidity: Provide moist air. Use a humidifier for best results.
Temperatures: 40° to 45° F at night, 60° to 65° F during the day.
Fertilization: Fertilize lightly throughout the growing season.
Propagation: Start new plants by dividing an old specimen.
Grooming: Pick off yellowed leaves.
Repotting: Repot at any time.
Problems: Leaves will scorch if plant is in a draft or dry air. Dry soil or a high level of soluble salts may damage roots, causing plant to die back.

Aglaonema
Chinese evergreen

Chinese evergreen, which can grow to 2 feet, is a favorite indoors because it tolerates a wide range of conditions, including poor light and dry air. Any number of common species and cultivars are available, including *A. modestum*, *A.* 'Silver Queen', *A. crispum*, and *A. commutatum*. Its oblong, lance-shaped leaves are 6 to 9 inches long and 2 to 3 inches wide. The leaves can be anything from entirely green to heavily marbled with silver and white. Creamy, waxy flowers like calla lilies bloom in late summer and early fall. Tight clusters of 1-inch-long, yellowish red berries follow the flowers. Growth slows during winter.
Light: Will survive in low (reading-level) light. Never place plant in direct sunlight.
Water: Keep evenly moist (somewhat drier in winter). Water thoroughly and discard drainage.
Humidity: Average indoor humidity levels.
Temperatures: 55° to 60° F at night, 70° to 75° F during the day.
Fertilization: Fertilize all year, more heavily in summer.

Aglaonema 'Silver Queen'

Alocasia 'African Mask'

Alpinia sanderae

Propagation: Take root divisions or stem cuttings in spring and summer. Seeds are available, but can be more difficult than divisions and cuttings.
Grooming: Remove yellowed leaves.
Repotting: Repot at any time. Blossoms best when pot bound.
Problems: Leaf edges will turn brown if level of soluble salts is too high or if plant is in a draft or dry air.

Alocasia
Alocasia

The striking foliage of the alocasia is arrow-shaped, often with lobed or wavy edges. Most varieties have shiny leaves, and some have a silvery overlay on much or part of the leaf. They grow from tubers, each producing a half dozen or so large leaves. Juvenile forms of alocasia are often quite small, but adult plants can reach 4 feet in height. The best known and most widely available is *Alocasia* × *amazonica,* which has dark green, almost black leaves and ivory veins. Several cultivars of this plant are available .
Light: Place in a bright, indirectly lit south, east, or west window.
Water: Water thoroughly, but allow to dry between waterings.
Humidity: Requires moist air. Use a humidifier for best results.
Temperatures: 65° to 70° F at night, 75° to 80° F during the day.
Fertilization: Fertilize lightly throughout the growing season.
Propagation: Divide in spring.
Grooming: Pick off yellowed leaves.
Repotting: Repot infrequently.
Problems: Subject to crown rot in overly moist conditions.

Alpinia sanderae
Variegated ginger

Its yellow to cream, feathered variegation and its modest stature in a genus of otherwise extremely tall plants has made the variegated ginger a popular houseplant in recent years. The thin canes with lance-shaped leaves arch away from the pot. For an attractive display, always plant 3 divisions to a pot, each stem facing in a different direction. The flowers are attractive but are rarely seen indoors.
Light: Provide at least 4 hours of curtain-filtered sunlight from a bright south, east, or west window.

Water: Water thoroughly, but allow to dry between waterings.
Humidity: Requires moist air. Use a humidifier for best results.
Temperatures: 65° to 70° F at night, 75° to 80° F during the day.
Fertilization: Fertilize lightly throughout the growing season.
Propagation: Divide in spring.
Grooming: Pick off yellowed leaves and cut out faded canes.
Repotting: Repot as necessary.
Problems: Subject to crown rot in overly moist conditions.

Anthurium
Anthurium

Although many attractive anthuriums are grown especially for their flowers, some are becoming increasingly popular as foliage plants. And with over 600 species in the wild in a bewildering variety of forms, there is an abundance to choose from. *A. crystallinum* is one that is often available. It has heart-shaped, emerald green leaves up to 12 inches across and 20 inches long, overlaid with attractive silver veins. *A. hookeri* 'Alicia' has thick, leathery dark green leaves with wavy edges and extremely short petioles that form a bird's nest rosette. *A. pedioradiatum* 'Fingers' bears shiny, broad leaves with finger-like, pointed projections. The latter two are especially tough and are well adapted to home care.
Light: Place in a bright, indirectly lit south, east, or west window.
Water: Water thoroughly, but allow to dry between waterings.
Humidity: Requires moist air. Use a humidifier for best results.
Temperatures: 65° to 70° F at night, 75° to 80° F during the day.
Fertilization: Fertilize lightly throughout the growing season.
Propagation: Remove and root offsets, or take cuttings from varieties with visible stems.
Grooming: Pick off yellowed leaves.
Repotting: Repot infrequently.
Problems: Subject to crown rot in overly moist conditions.

Araucaria heterophylla
Norfolk Island pine, bunya-bunya

Norfolk Island pine is popular for indoor use because of its formal, treelike appearance. It grows slowly indoors, so you may prefer to purchase a mature specimen. A related plant, *A. bidwillii* (bunya-bunya), has a less formal shape, with sharp needles in two rows along its stem, and also grows indoors. Norfolk Island pine resembles a fir tree and can be decorated at Christmastime.

Light: Provide at least moderate light but no direct sunlight.

Water: Keep evenly moist. Water thoroughly and discard drainage.

Humidity: Average indoor humidity levels.

Temperatures: 50° to 55° F at night, 65° to 70° F during the day.

Fertilization: Fertilize lightly throughout the growing season.

Propagation: Home propagation is not practical.

Grooming: Pick off yellowed leaves.

Repotting: Repot infrequently.

Problems: Leaves will scorch if plant is in a draft or dry air. Poor drainage, too-frequent watering, or standing in water will cause root rot. Leaves will drop if soil is too wet or too dry.

Asparagus
Asparagus fern

Two of the most popular asparagus ferns are *A. densiflorus* 'Sprengeri', which has arching 18- to 24-inch stems covered with thousands of 1-inch, flat needles, and *A. setaceus*, a trailing vine with 12- to 18-inch stems covered with dark green, ⅛-inch needles. Both look best in hanging baskets. A third variety, also popular, is *A. densiflorus* 'Myers', which has stiff, upright stems to 2 feet and dark green, needle leaves, which give it an airy, feathery look.

These plants have been favorites for generations because they are so easy to care for. Unlike true ferns, they tolerate a wide range of temperatures and light, do not require a humid atmosphere, and can be propagated easily. To keep the plants bushy, pinch back their long stems periodically.

Light: Provide bright indirect or curtain-filtered sunlight.

Water: Water thoroughly, but allow to dry between waterings.

Humidity: Average indoor humidity levels.

Temperatures: 60° to 65° F at night, 68° to 72° F during the day.

Fertilization: Fertilize lightly throughout the growing season.

Anthurium crystallinum

Anthurium hookeri

Araucaria heterophylla

Asparagus densiflorus 'Sprengeri'

Aspidistra elatior 'Variegata'

Aucuba japonica 'Picturata'

Bamboo: *Arundinaria pygmaea*

Propagation: Divide thick roots of old plants in any season.
Grooming: Pinch back stems to keep bushy; if plant gets leggy, cut stems to soil level. Fresh new stems will soon begin to grow.
Repotting: Repot any time plant becomes overcrowded.
Problems: Leaves will turn yellow and drop if plant is suddenly moved to a location with low light.

Aspidistra elatior
Cast-iron plant

This tough plant was one of the most popular houseplants of the Victorian era. It's a tough plant; it can survive extreme heat and low light that would be deadly to most other plants. Its leaves are oblong, shiny, dark green, and leathery, growing 15 to 30 inches long and 3 to 4 inches wide. They intermingle above a clump of 6-inch stems. In spring, dark purple, bell-shaped flowers are borne singly at the soil surface.

This slow-growing, long-lasting plant responds well to proper attention, but it can survive poor treatment for a long time. Place out of direct sun, in average warmth and a moderately bright and well-ventilated room, and water regularly from spring to fall. Reduce water and keep the plant cool during winter, when it rests. Although it can withstand most types of abuse, this plant cannot endure soggy soil or frequent repotting.
Light: Will survive in low (reading-level) light.
Water: Water thoroughly, but allow to dry between waterings. In winter, keep plant dry and water infrequently.
Humidity: Dry air is generally not harmful, but keep plant out of drafts.
Temperatures: 50° to 55° F at night, 60° to 65° F during the day.
Fertilization: Fertilize lightly throughout the growing season.
Propagation: Start new plants by dividing an old specimen.
Grooming: Pick off yellowed leaves.
Repotting: Can be repotted at any time, but infrequent repotting is best.
Problems: Poor drainage, too-frequent watering, or standing in water will cause root rot. Susceptible to spider mites. Will not withstand frequent repotting.

Aucuba japonica
Japanese aucuba, golddust-tree

Aucubas are woody shrubs grown outdoors in many climates. The various cultivars have yellow variegation patterns or speckles on shiny, green leaves when grown in bright light. Keep the plants cool at night and out of direct sunlight during the day. Be careful not to overfertilize. Prune in early spring to train into a bushy plant.
Light: Provide at least 4 hours of curtain-filtered sunlight from a bright south, east, or west window.
Water: Let soil get almost dry before watering, then water thoroughly and discard drainage.
Humidity: Average indoor humidity levels.
Temperatures: 40° to 45° F at night, 60° to 65° F during the day.
Fertilization: Fertilize lightly throughout the growing season.
Propagation: Take root cuttings at any time.
Grooming: Prune in early spring.
Repotting: Repot in winter or early spring, as needed.
Problems: Poor drainage, too-frequent watering, or standing in water will cause root rot. Dry soil or a high level of soluble salts may damage roots, causing plant to die back.

Bamboo

Several genera of plants are known as bamboo, including *Bambusa, Phyllostachys,* and *Arundinaria. A. pygmaea* (formerly known as *Sasa pygmaea*) is tolerant of most indoor conditions. It is a dwarf, growing only to about 1 foot, but many other bamboos are large plants that grow rapidly, given enough warmth and moisture. Bamboo can work well in an interior design because of its columnar shape; for example, at a window, it can frame or partially obscure a view.
Light: Provide 4 hours or more of direct sunlight from a south window.
Water: Keep very moist at all times, but do not allow to stand in water.
Humidity: Provide moist air. Use a humidifier for best results.
Temperatures: 55° to 60° F at night, 70° to 75° F during the day.
Fertilization: Fertilize all year, more heavily in summer.

Propagation: Take cuttings from rhizomes or underground stems at any time.
Grooming: Cut back and thin out old shoots at any time.
Repotting: Repot infrequently.
Problems: No serious problems.

Begonia

There are thousands of begonia species, hybrids, and cultivars. Most of the ones mentioned in this book are popular as flowering plants, but some are more useful and attractive as foliage plants. Even these will produce small flowers on long, graceful stalks if given enough light. These plants often do well outdoors on a shaded patio during summer.

Cultivars of foliage begonias are usually selected for the color, shape, and variegation of the foliage. Because many have shades of red or maroon in the foliage, a plant light (bluish purple) will greatly enhance the brightness of the leaf colors. In fact, foliage begonias altogether thrive under lights. For best results, keep these begonias warm and avoid crown rot by never overwatering.

Cane begonias
Angel-wing begonia

The leaves of cane begonias are borne vertically on erect, smooth stems with swollen nodes somewhat like those of bamboo. They are asymmetrical and quite diverse in color, size, and variegation. The plants are not normally self-branching, but instead send up new stems from the base. Many cultivars grow quite large and need plenty of room. Although grown primarily for their foliage, they will bloom intermittently throughout the year if given enough light.

Best known are the angel-wing begonias, which have large leaves, silver-spotted on top and red underneath. The old-fashioned hybrid B. corallina 'Lucerna' (or 'Corallina de Lucerna') is the most common angel-wing. It bears coral flowers and can reach over 4 feet at maturity. B. coccinea is similar but of intermediate height. Some, such as B. 'Orange Rubra', are pendulous in habit, making them good choices for hanging baskets. Others, such as B. 'Sophie Cecile', are upright in growth and have deeply cut leaves.

Light: Provide bright but indirect light from a south, east, or west window.
Water: Let plant approach dryness before watering, then water thoroughly and discard drainage.
Humidity: Average indoor humidity levels.
Temperatures: 65° to 70° F at night, 75°F to 80° F during the day.
Fertilization: Fertilize lightly throughout the growing season.
Propagation: Take stem cuttings at any time.
Grooming: Cut back long stems to promote new growth.
Repotting: Repot annually in spring for best growth.
Problems: Subject to crown rot in overly moist conditions.

Rhizomatous begonias
Iron-cross begonia, beefsteak begonia, lettuceleaf begonia, eyelash begonia, star begonia

The rhizomatous begonias are the largest group of begonias. Their jointed rhizomes grow along or under the soil surface and hang over the edge of the pot. The rhizomes are not attractive, but generally they are hidden from view by the plant foliage, which is often attractively mottled and textured. In ample light, many rhizomatous begonias bear tall stalks of white or greenish white flowers held well above the leaves. B. masoniana (iron-cross begonia) is one of the best known of this group; it produces large, bumpy, heart-shaped leaves in yellow-green with a dark burgundy, Maltese-cross pattern in the center. Some old-fashioned hybrids with thick rhizomes and extralarge leaves are still popular, such as B. × erythrophylla (beefsteak begonia), with round, shiny bronze leaves, and B. erythrophylla 'Bunchii' (lettuceleaf begonia), with highly crested leaf edges. More popular these days, though, are the smaller varieties, such as the tiny B. boweri (eyelash begonia), the larger B. heracleifolia (star begonia), and the numerous intermediate hybrids, such as B. 'Maphil', B. 'Chantilly Lace', and B. 'Bow-Nigra'. Some of the small rhizomatous begonias need high humidity and are best grown in terrariums. One of these is B. prismatocarpa, which bears bright buttercup yellow flowers throughout the year.

Begonia 'Mandarin Orange' (Cane begonia)

Begonia masoniana (Rhizomatous begonia)

Begonia luxurians (Shrub begonia)

Begonia × rex-cultorum 'Cleopatra'

Brassaia actinophylla

Light: Provide bright but indirect light from a south, east, or west window.
Water: Let plant approach dryness before watering, then water thoroughly and discard drainage.
Humidity: Provide moist air. Use a humidifier for best results.
Temperatures: 65° to 70° F at night, 75° to 80° F during the day.
Fertilization: Fertilize lightly throughout the growing season.
Propagation: Take leaf or rhizome cuttings at any time.
Grooming: Shape with pruning or clipping at any time. Excessively long rhizomes can be cut back.
Repotting: Repot infrequently.
Problems: Subject to crown rot in overly moist conditions. Will not bloom if light is too low.

Shrub begonias
Trout-leaf begonia

Shrub begonias branch abundantly, hiding their stems from view. Unlike many cane begonias, however, they tend to flower only seasonally and so are grown almost exclusively for their foliage. The bare-leaf types have smooth, metallic-looking leaves; the old-fashioned bare-leaf hybrid *B. × thurstonii* has bronze-green leaves with a red underside that are remarkably reflective. The trout-leaf begonia, *B. × argenteo-guttata,* is also in the bare-leaf category, although its silver-spotted leaves make it resemble a miniature angel-wing begonia. Bare-leaf begonias generally require more sunlight than other begonias. Another type of shrub begonia has leaves covered in thick hair or felt. *B. scharffiana,* for example, has bronze-green leaves dusted with white hair. Hairy-leaf begonias prefer diffuse light. The fern-leaf begonias are best known for their unusual foliage: *B. foliosa* has tiny, ovate leaves that liberally coat its arching stems, and *B. luxurians* has giant leaves that are divided into narrow leaflets attached together at the base like spokes on a wheel.
Light: For hairy-leaf begonias, provide bright but indirect light from a south, east, or west window. Give bare-leaf begonias some direct sunlight.
Water: Let plant approach dryness before watering, then water thoroughly and discard drainage.
Humidity: Average indoor humidity levels.

Temperatures: 65° to 70° F at night, 75° to 80° F during the day.
Fertilization: Fertilize lightly throughout the growing season.
Propagation: Take stem cuttings at any time.
Grooming: Cut back long stems to promote branching.
Repotting: Repot annually in spring for best growth.
Problems: Subject to crown rot in overly moist conditions.

Begonia × rex-cultorum
Rex begonia

Rex begonias are a sizable group of plants grown primarily for their foliage. They will bloom if given good light, producing tiny flowers on long stems. The leaves of most cultivars are large and have asymmetrical blades with diverse, brilliant coloration and textures. The rex begonias are rhizomatous in habit; their stems may grow horizontally across the soil surface. Keep them warm and take care not to overwater. Fertilize lightly.
Light: Provide bright but indirect light from a south, east, or west window.
Water: Let plant approach dryness before watering, then water thoroughly and discard drainage.
Humidity: Average indoor humidity levels.
Temperatures: 65° to 70° F at night, 75° to 80° F during the day.
Fertilization: Fertilize lightly throughout the growing season.
Propagation: Take rhizome or leaf cuttings at any time. Seeds are available, but can be more difficult than cuttings.
Grooming: Keep to desired height and shape with light pruning or clipping at any time. Give plant plenty of room.
Repotting: Repot infrequently.
Problems: Subject to crown rot in overly moist conditions.

Brassaia
Schefflera, umbrella tree

Scheffleras are often used in commercial settings because they grow fast and are relatively easy to care for. *B. actinophylla,* although sold as a small seedling, can become huge. Its leaves are palmately compound and may be a foot or more across, spreading out like the sections of an umbrella. *B. actinophylla* 'Amate' has become a popular choice within the past few years. For information on the miniature schefflera, sometimes listed as *B. arboricola,* see *Heptapleurum arboricola.*

Light: Provide bright but indirect light from a south, east, or west window.
Water: Let plant approach dryness before watering, then water thoroughly and discard drainage.
Humidity: Average indoor humidity levels.
Temperatures: 50° to 55° F at night, 60° to 65° F during the day.
Fertilization: Fertilize lightly throughout the growing season.
Propagation: Take stem cuttings at any time. Seeds are available, but can be more difficult than cuttings.
Grooming: Give plant plenty of room. Pick off yellowed leaves.
Repotting: Repot infrequently.
Problems: Will get spindly and weak if light is too low. Leaves will drop if soil is too wet or too dry. Spider mites can be a problem, especially if air is too dry.

Buxus
Boxwood

Boxwood is a woody shrub found in many outdoor gardens. It can easily be made into a formal hedge. Many boxwoods are becoming popular as indoor plants, especially for bonsai. They have a dense branching habit, resulting in thick masses of tiny, green leaves. They can be cut and pruned to almost any shape. Keep boxwoods cool at night and do not overwater or overfertilize.

Light: Provide at least 4 hours of curtain-filtered sunlight from a bright south, east, or west window.
Water: Let plant approach dryness before watering, then water thoroughly and discard drainage.
Humidity: Average indoor humidity levels.
Temperatures: 50° to 55° F at night, 60° to 65° F during the day.
Fertilization: Fertilize lightly throughout the growing season.
Propagation: Take cuttings from stems or shoots that have recently matured.
Grooming: Keep to desired height and shape with light pruning or clipping at any time.

Repotting: Repot infrequently.
Problems: Dry soil or a high level of soluble salts may damage roots, causing plant to die back. Spider mites can be a problem, especially if air is too dry.

Caladium
Caladium

Caladiums, with their dozens of different leaf patterns and colors, can create a display of color to rival that of any flowering plant. Masses of exquisite paper-thin, heart-shaped leaves, 12 to 24 inches long, are borne on long stalks. The plant is perennial yet dies back for a 4-month period during winter. *C. bicolor* features wide, red leaves bordered with green that are 14 inches long and 6½ inches wide. *C. humboldtii* is a miniature plant; its light green leaves are splotched with white.

Light: Provide at least 4 hours of curtain-filtered sunlight from a bright south, east, or west window.
Water: Keep evenly moist, although plant can tolerate some dryness between waterings. Allow to dry out and become dormant in fall.
Humidity: Provide moist air. Use a humidifier for best results.
Temperatures: 55° to 60° F at night, 70° to 75° F during the day.
Fertilization: Fertilize lightly throughout the growing season.
Propagation: Start new plants from the bulblets that develop beside the parent bulb. Pot these bulblets in late winter, when plant is dormant.
Grooming: Remove old leaves as plant goes dormant.
Repotting: Repot each year.
Problems: Leaves will scorch if plant is in a draft or dry air. Plant will get spindly and weak if light is too low.

Calathea
Calathea, peacock-plant

Calatheas have what many consider to be the most beautifully variegated foliage of any indoor plant. The stems are often red, and the large, blade leaves have various patterns of greens on top. Some cultivars have purples and reds on the undersides of the leaves. Calatheas will not tolerate dry air or drafts; they are often grown in lit terrariums. Give the plants plenty of room, since they can grow 2 feet high, with individual leaves 8 inches across.

Buxus sempervirens 'Suffruticosa'

Caladium 'Red Flash'

Calathea louisae

Chlorophytum comosum 'Vittatum'

Cissus antarctica

Light: Will survive in low (reading-level) light.
Water: Keep very moist at all times, but do not allow to stand in water.
Humidity: Provide moist air. Use a humidifier for best results.
Temperatures: 65° to 70° F at night, 75° to 80° F during the day.
Fertilization: Fertilize lightly once a year in early spring if plant is in a dimly lit spot. Otherwise, fertilize lightly throughout the growing season.
Propagation: Start plants by dividing an old specimen.
Grooming: Pick off yellowed leaves.
Repotting: Repot at any time.
Problems: Leaves will scorch if plant is in a draft or dry air. Dry soil or a high level of soluble salts may damage roots, causing plant to die back.

Chlorophytum comosum
Spiderplant

The familiar spiderplant has been grown indoors for nearly 200 years, when Goethe, the German writer and philosopher, brought the plant inside because he was fascinated by its habit of producing miniature plants on shoots. The spiderplant can grow to be 3 feet tall. Wiry stems up to 5 feet long, bearing plantlets, spring forth among grassy, green, arching leaves striped with yellow or white. This plant is perfect for a hanging basket.

The spiderplant will grow in almost any location—sunny or shady, dry or damp. Water freely from spring to autumn, and keep in a moderate to cool location. Feed every other week. The plantlets can be left on the stems of the parent plant for a full look, or they can be removed for propagation. The plant will produce the most plantlets when slightly pot bound.
Light: Provide at least moderate light but no direct sunlight.
Water: Keep very moist during growth and flowering; at other times, allow to dry between waterings.
Humidity: Average indoor humidity levels.
Temperatures: 50° to 55° F at night, 60° to 65° F during the day.
Fertilization: Fertilize all year, more heavily in summer.
Propagation: Remove plantlets or rooted side shoots as they form.
Grooming: Give plant plenty of room to grow.

Repotting: Repot in winter or early spring as needed.
Problems: Brown leaf tips can be caused by a high level of soluble salts. Dry soil or soluble salts may damage roots, causing plant to die back.

Cissus

Cissus is a member of the grape family, a trailing or vining plant that becomes woodier with age. It is attractive in hanging baskets or trained onto a trellis. Of all the genera in the grape family, *Cissus* is the one most suitable for indoor culture, given moderate light and dry air. Several species are mentioned here. Although their culture is similar, enough differences exist to warrant individual care guides.

Cissus is popular in commercial settings. The plants also grow rapidly in the home and acclimate easily to poor light and infrequent watering. With care, plants can be maintained for many months in adverse conditions, but they will not flourish unless they are given bright indirect or even full sunlight and kept moderately moist and well fertilized. Prune stem tips and train the vines frequently to encourage plant to grow in an attractive shape.

Cissus antarctica
Kangaroo-ivy, kangaroo vine

Kangaroo-ivy is a vigorous indoor climber, an obvious member of the grape family. It is usually trained onto a trellis, string, or post, but can be used also in hanging baskets. The foliage is large and shiny, but may be sparse along the stem if the plant is not in good light. To counter a spindly appearance, many indoor gardeners train or wrap several vines together to make the foliage look denser.
Light: Provide at least moderate light but no direct sunlight.
Water: Let plant approach dryness before watering, then water thoroughly and discard drainage.
Humidity: Average indoor humidity levels.
Temperatures: 50° to 55° F at night, 65° to 70° F during the day.
Fertilization: Fertilize lightly throughout the growing season.
Propagation: Take stem cuttings at any time.

Grooming: Keep to desired height and shape with light pruning or clipping at any time.
Repotting: Repot at any time.
Problems: Will get spindly and weak if light is too low.

Cissus discolor
Begonia-treebine

Begonia-treebine is a vigorous vine that will grow to 6 feet or more unless pruned. It needs more light than its cousins kangaroo-ivy and grape-ivy. The leaves resemble those of a rex begonia, velvety with toothed edges and red veins. In ample light, pink and white colorations will appear.
Light: Provide 4 hours or more of direct sunlight from a south window.
Water: Keep evenly moist. Water thoroughly and discard drainage.
Humidity: Requires moist air. Use a humidifier for best results.
Temperatures: 55° to 60° F at night, 70° to 75° F during the day.
Fertilization: Fertilize all year, more heavily in summer.
Propagation: Take stem cuttings at any time.
Grooming: Keep to desired height and shape with light pruning or clipping at any time.
Repotting: Repot in winter or early spring as needed.
Problems: Will get spindly and weak if light is too low.

Cissus rhombifolia
Grape-ivy, oakleaf ivy

Grape-ivy grows wild in the West Indies and South America. It is a grape family vining plant best grown in a hanging basket. Its stems and buds are brown and have reddish hairs, and its shiny, 3-leaflet leaves are similar to those of poison ivy. Its two cultivars, 'Mandaiana' and 'Ellen Danica', are grown most often. Grape-ivy is popular with indoor gardeners because it tolerates a wide range of growing conditions and grows rapidly, even in moderate light.
Light: Will survive in low (reading-level) light.
Water: Let plant approach dryness before watering, then water thoroughly and discard drainage.
Humidity: Dry air is generally not harmful, but keep plant out of drafts.

Temperatures: 50° to 55° F at night, 60° to 65° F during the day.
Fertilization: Fertilize lightly throughout the growing season.
Propagation: Take stem cuttings at any time.
Grooming: Keep to desired height and shape with light pruning or clipping at any time.
Repotting: Repot at any time.
Problems: Leaves will drop if soil is too wet or too dry. Dry soil or a high level of soluble salts may damage roots, causing plant to die back. Powdery mildew occurs occasionally.

Clusia rosea
Balsam-apple

Balsam-apple is an attractive indoor tree with extremely thick, spoon-shaped leaves measuring up to 8 inches long and 4 inches wide. It takes up a great deal of space if allowed to grow to its natural height and spread, but regular pruning will keep it under control. The pink to white flowers are rarely borne indoors.
Light: Place in a bright, indirectly lit south, east, or west window.
Water: Water thoroughly, but allow to dry between waterings.
Humidity: Average indoor humidity levels.
Temperatures: 65° to 70° F at night, 75° to 80° F during the day.
Fertilization: Fertilize lightly throughout the growing season.
Propagation: Take stem cuttings in spring.
Grooming: Pick off yellowed leaves. Prune as needed.
Repotting: Repot infrequently.
Problems: Lower leaves drop as plant ages.

Codiaeum variegatum
Croton, Joseph's coat

The varied leaf shapes and exotic leaf colors of the croton make it an especially attractive indoor plant. Growing to 3 feet high, it produces lance-shaped, leathery leaves that reach up to 18 inches long. Foliage colors of the many varieties include red, pink, orange, brown, and white. Color markings vary considerably among leaves on the same plant. In addition, the plant may change color as it matures.

Cissus discolor

Cissus rhombifolia

Codiaeum variegatum var. *pictum*

Coffea arabica

Coleus × *hybridus*

Cordyline terminalis 'Kiwi'

C. variegatum var. *pictum* (Joseph's-coat) is a popular croton. Its oval, lobed leaves somewhat resemble oak leaves, and it grows as a narrow shrub that usually attains a height of 2 to 4 feet.

Crotons are not easy to grow unless you can satisfy all their environmental needs. Plenty of sunshine and a warm, draft-free location are essential. The key to success is keeping the air humid enough so that the plant can cope with the sun and warm temperatures. Place it on a humidifying tray to ensure adequate moisture. Dry air or dry soil will cause the leaves to wither rapidly and die.

Light: Provide 4 hours or more of direct sunlight from a south window.
Water: Keep evenly moist. Water thoroughly and discard drainage.
Humidity: Requires moist air. Use a humidifying tray for best results.
Temperatures: 65° to 70° F at night, 75° to 80° F during the day.
Fertilization: Fertilize lightly throughout the growing season.
Propagation: Take cuttings from stems or shoots before they have hardened or matured. Or propagate by air layering.
Grooming: Clean leaves and inspect for pests regularly. Pinching or pruning occasionally will cause plant to branch and become fuller.
Repotting: Repot in winter or early spring as needed.
Problems: Leaves will scorch if plant is in a draft or dry air. They will drop if soil is too wet or too dry. Susceptible to spider mites.

Coffea arabica
Coffee plant

Is it possible to grow your own coffee in the living room? Actually, coffee plants tend not to flower indoors, but they do make attractive, bushy shrubs up to 3 or more feet in height. The dark green, elliptic leaves have wavy margins. Keep pruned for a bushy look.

Light: Place in a bright, indirectly lit south, east, or west window.
Water: Water thoroughly, but allow to dry between waterings.
Humidity: Requires moist air. Use a humidifier for best results.
Temperatures: 55° to 60° F at night, 65° to 70° F during the day.
Fertilization: Fertilize lightly throughout the growing season.

Propagation: Start new plants from unroasted coffee beans or from cuttings.
Grooming: Pick off yellowed leaves. Prune and pinch as needed.
Repotting: Repot annually in spring for best growth.
Problems: May lose inner and lower leaves if soil is too moist or too dry. Maintain high air humidity to prevent spider mites.

Coleus × *hybridus*
Coleus

Coleus is a fast-growing, tropical shrub. So richly colored are its leaves that many people choose it as a colorful, inexpensive substitute for croton. The velvety, oval, scalloped leaves taper to a point and come in a multitude of colors with toothed or fringed margins, depending on the variety. Dark blue or white flowers form in fall.

Light: Place in a bright, indirectly lit south, east, or west window.
Water: Keep evenly moist. Water thoroughly and discard drainage.
Humidity: Average indoor humidity levels.
Temperatures: 55° to 60° F at night, 70° to 75° F during the day.
Fertilization: Fertilize only when plant is growing actively.
Propagation: Take stem cuttings at any time.
Grooming: Prune in early spring. Pinch back stem tips of young or regrowing plants to improve form.
Repotting: Repot each year.
Problems: Some leaf drop will occur in winter. Will get spindly and weak if light is too low.

Cordyline terminalis
Cordyline, Hawaiian ti

Cordylines are large outdoor plants in their native South Sea Islands. The narrow leaves, which can be 18 inches long, are often used for hula skirts. Popular indoor cultivars will grow to about 3 feet and have foliage with pink variegations and stripes along the leaf edges. Although cordylines will tolerate low light, foliage color will not develop well under such conditions. For a more interesting look, use several plants to a pot. Cordyline is difficult to grow to perfection indoors because of its need for extremely humid air.

Light: Will survive in low (reading-level) light.

Water: Let plant approach dryness before watering, then water thoroughly and discard drainage.

Humidity: Requires moist air. Use a humidifier for best results.

Temperatures: 65° to 70° F at night, 75° to 80° F during the day.

Fertilization: Fertilize lightly throughout the growing season.

Propagation: Take stem cuttings at any time. Or start new plants by air layering.

Grooming: Pick off yellowed leaves.

Repotting: Repot at any time.

Problems: Leaves will scorch if plant is in a draft or dry air. Spider mites can be a problem, especially if air is too dry.

Cycas revoluta
Fern-palm, sago palm

Although fern-palm resembles a palm tree, it is more closely related to modern conifers. The leaves are shiny and extremely stiff. Although they appear tough, they are actually quite easily damaged, and since the plant produces only one new set of leaves each year, any damage remains visible for a long time. The plant forms a trunk like a palm trunk, but only after many years' growth. Fern-palm is very slow growing; if you want a plant with a trunk, buy one that has already reached that stage. Other types of cycads occasionally grown indoors include *Ceratozamia, Dioon, Encephalartos,* and *Zamia.*

Light: Provide at least 4 hours of curtain-filtered sunlight from a south, east, or west window.

Water: Water thoroughly, but allow to dry between waterings.

Humidity: Requires moist air. Use a humidifier for best results.

Temperatures: 55° to 60° F at night, 70° to 75° F during the day.

Fertilization: Fertilize lightly in spring and summer.

Propagation: Growing from seed is a slow process best left to professionals. Offsets are unlikely under home conditions.

Grooming: Pick off yellowed leaves.

Repotting: Repot infrequently.

Problems: Spider mites can be a problem if air is dry.

Cyperus
Umbrella plant, pygmy papyrus

Cyperus papyrus, which is common in the Middle East, was used historically to make the writing material known as papyrus. The long, green stems bear whorls of leaves, resembling the spokes of an umbrella. These "leaves" are actually bracts, among which small green to brown flowers appear. Dwarf cultivars are available as small plants, but most soon grow to 2 to 4 feet. The most popular species used indoors is *C. alternifolius.* Cyperus is a member of the sedge family. Like all the sedges, it is semiaquatic and likes wet conditions, preferring to stand in water at all times. The leaves may scorch or burn in dry indoor air. Tall plants may require staking.

Light: In winter, keep in about 4 hours of direct sunlight. In summer, provide curtain-filtered sunlight from a south or west window.

Water: Keep very moist at all times. Can stand in water.

Humidity: Requires moist air. Use a humidifier for best results.

Temperatures: 40° to 45° F at night, 60° to 65° F during the day.

Fertilization: Fertilize lightly throughout the growing season.

Propagation: Start new plants by dividing an old specimen. Or start from seed, but seeds are more difficult than division. *C. alternifolius* is most easily propagated from cuttings of leaf clusters.

Grooming: Pick off yellowed leaves.

Repotting: Repot in winter or early spring as needed.

Problems: Spider mites can be a problem, especially if air is too dry. Leaves will scorch if plant is in a draft or dry air.

Dieffenbachia
Dieffenbachia, dumb-cane

When touched by the tongue, sap from the cane stems of dieffenbachia can cause temporary speechlessness and much pain, hence the name "dumb-cane." This handsome evergreen features a single, thick trunk when young; as it matures it can be potted with multiple trunks together to form a palmlike appearance. Mature plants reach ceiling height. They have few equals for

Cycas revoluta

Cyperus alternifolius

Dieffenbachia 'Tropic Snow'

Dionaea muscipula

Dizygotheca elegantissima

planter and large container decorations. Arching, oblong, pointed leaves, 10 to 12 inches long, spiral around the trunk. *D. maculata* 'Rudolph Roehrs' has chartreuse leaves marbled with ivory and divided by a dark green central rib. The newer hybrids, 'Tropic Snow' and 'Camile', are clumping and stay compact longer than the older varieties.

Light: Will survive in low (reading-level) light, but prefers a moderately bright spot such as a north or east window.

Water: Water thoroughly, but allow to dry between waterings.

Humidity: Average indoor humidity levels.

Temperatures: 50° to 55° F at night, 65° to 70° F during the day.

Fertilization: Fertilize all year, more heavily in summer.

Propagation: Take stem cuttings or air-layer at any time.

Grooming: Pick off yellowed leaves and wash leaves occasionally.

Repotting: Repot at any time.

Problems: Poor drainage, too-frequent watering, or standing in water will cause root rot.

Dionaea muscipula
Venus's-flytrap

Venus's-flytrap is a carnivorous plant grown as a curiosity; it's especially popular with young children. The leaf tips are divided into traps that close on flies and other small insects or when touched with a finger. It really does not need to be fed indoors, but occasional insects can be supplied. Never give it red meat of any kind. It is also unwise to stimulate the traps too often, as they die after responding only a few times.

Venus's-flytrap is relatively easy to grow for short periods indoors, but hard to keep from one year to the next because its cultural needs are difficult to meet indoors. It is best grown in a terrarium. It goes into dormancy in winter and requires cool conditions at that time. Remove flower stems as they weaken the plant needlessly.

Other carnivorous plants that will grow indoors under similar conditions include *Drosera* (sundew), *Darlingtonia californica* (cobraplant), and tropical *Nepenthes* (pitcher plant).

Light: Provide at least 4 hours of curtain-filtered sunlight from a south, east, or west window.

Water: Keep evenly moist except during winter dormancy. Use only rain or distilled water.

Humidity: Requires very moist air. Does best in a terrarium.

Temperatures: 45° to 50° F at night, 55° to 60° F during the day. During dormancy, near-freezing temperatures (under 40° F) are preferred.

Fertilization: Do not fertilize. Feed occasionally with insects.

Propagation: Propagate by division or leaf cuttings in spring.

Grooming: Pick off blackened leaves.

Repotting: Repot each spring into pure sphagnum moss.

Problems: Subject to crown rot if conditions are too warm.

Dizygotheca elegantissima
False-aralia

False-aralia is one of the most graceful plants you can grow indoors. Thin, dark green leaves with lighter veins spread into nine fingers with saw-toothed edges. You can buy small seedlings for a terrarium or a mature plant large enough to sit under. The leaves of mature plants have a decidedly different look from the juvenile leaves.

With proper care, this slow grower should cause few problems. It is, however, extremely sensitive to soil moisture and won't tolerate either soggy soil or a dry rootball. Don't move it around often; it does best when kept in the same location. Moist air is another important factor in keeping it healthy.

Light: Place in a bright, indirectly lit south, east, or west window. Older plants can endure less light.

Water: Keep evenly moist. Water thoroughly and discard drainage. In winter, keep plant almost dry, watering infrequently.

Humidity: Average indoor humidity levels.

Temperatures: 55° to 60° F at night, 70° to 75° F during the day.

Fertilization: Fertilize lightly throughout the growing season.

Propagation: Difficult to propagate. Try sowing seeds in a small pot and transplant seedlings as necessary.

Grooming: Keep to desired height and shape with light pruning or clipping at any time.

Repotting: Repot infrequently, in winter or early spring when needed.

Problems: Leaves will drop if soil is too wet or too dry. Spider mites can be a problem, especially if air is too dry.

Dracaena

Dracaenas usually have tall stems like palm trees, with tufts of narrow, sword-like leaves near the top. Most grow into large plants, often 10 feet or more in height. To offset its natural tendency for tall, leggy growth, stems of different heights are often planted together in the same pot or the stems are contorted to achieve different heights. Many indoor gardeners air-layer the plants to reduce their height. The canes that are left after the air layers are removed will usually sprout new leafy growth.

Many dracaena varieties are available. Most are selected for their foliage and form, used for large-scale architectural plantings indoors. Some have narrow, spiky foliage; others have wider, more arching leaves. Most of the popular cultivars are variegated. *D. fragrans* 'Massangeana' occasionally produces sprays of extremely fragrant, white flowers among its large leaves. In many commercial interiors these flowers are removed because their aroma is overpowering.

If conditioned properly, dracaenas will tolerate low light and infrequent watering; but they will grow little, if at all, under such conditions. Because their care depends somewhat on the cultivar chosen, an individual care guide is given for each species.

Dracaena deremensis
Warneckii dracaena,
Janet Craig dracaena

Warneckii and Janet Craig dracaenas grow as single-stemmed plants with long, narrow leaves arching outward all along the stem. It is common to cluster several plants of differing heights in one pot to give more visual interest. 'Janet Craig', the larger of the two, has dark green, shiny leaves and will grow to 5 or 6 feet if given ample light. A dwarf cultivar, 'Janet Craig Compacta', is also available. 'Warneckii' has narrower leaves with thin, white stripes along the leaf edges. These dracaenas are quite tolerant of stressful indoor environments, but avoid overwatering or overfertilizing plants that are growing in low light to keep them at their best.

Light: 'Warneckii' will survive in low (reading-level) light. 'Janet Craig' needs moderate or bright light. Neither will tolerate direct sunlight.
Water: Let plant approach dryness before watering, then water thoroughly and discard drainage.
Humidity: Average indoor humidity levels.
Temperatures: 55° to 60° F at night, 70° to 75° F during the day.
Fertilization: Fertilize all year, more heavily in summer.
Propagation: Take stem cuttings at any time, or start new plants by air layering.
Grooming: Pick off yellowed leaves. Trim brown leaf tips.
Repotting: Repot at any time.
Problems: Leaves will drop if soil is too wet or too dry. Leaf tips will turn brown from excessively dry potting mix or a high level of soluble salts.

Dracaena fragrans 'Massangeana'
Cornplant

The leaves of the cornplant are long and narrow, although broader than those of *D. deremensis,* with a yellow stripe down the center, resembling corn leaves. The plant is grown in two ways: as a single stem with leaves reaching outward all along the trunk, or as a series of bare stems that have been topped to produce clusters of foliage on stalks that sprout from the cuts. In ample light, the cornplant may occasionally produce an extremely fragrant flower. It can tolerate many abuses, but be careful not to overwater or overfertilize a plant growing in low light.
Light: Will survive in low (reading-level) light.
Water: Let plant approach dryness before watering, then water thoroughly and discard drainage.
Humidity: Average indoor humidity levels.
Temperatures: 55° to 60° F at night, 70° to 75° F during the day.
Fertilization: Fertilize all year, more heavily in summer.
Propagation: Take stem cuttings at any time, or start new plants by air layering.
Grooming: Pick off yellowed leaves. Trim brown leaf tips.
Repotting: Repot at any time.

Dracaena deremensis 'Janet Craig'

Dracaena deremensis 'Warneckii'

Dracaena fragrans 'Massangeana'

Dracaena marginata 'Colorama'

Dracaena reflexa 'Song of Jamaica'

Dracaena sanderana

Problems: Leaves will drop if soil is too wet or too dry. Leaf tips will turn brown from excessively dry potting mix or a high level of soluble salts.

Dracaena marginata
Madagascar dragontree,
red-margined dracaena

Dracaena marginata has the narrowest leaves of all the commonly grown dracaenas. All cultivars have red striping on the edges of the leaves; 'Tricolor' and 'Colorama' are striped lengthwise in pink or cream but need more light and humidity than the species to do well indoors. The plants are normally grown as a series of stems with the foliage at the top. As the plants grow, the older leaves will yellow and die back, but the older stems may branch at the top. Avoid leaf tip burn by keeping the plant evenly moist and out of drafts.
Light: Provide at least moderate light but no direct sunlight.
Water: Keep evenly moist. Water thoroughly and discard drainage.
Humidity: Average indoor humidity levels.
Temperatures: 55° to 60° F at night, 70° to 75° F during the day.
Fertilization: Fertilize lightly throughout the growing season.
Propagation: Take stem cuttings at any time, or start new plants by air layering.
Grooming: Pick off yellowed leaves. Trim leaves with brown tips.
Repotting: Repot at any time.
Problems: Leaves will scorch if plant is in a draft or dry air. Watch for spider mites, especially if air is dry.

Dracaena reflexa
Pleomele

Pleomele, until recently classified as *Pleomele reflexa*, grows into a large plant with reflexed, or downward-pointing, leaves closely set along cane-like stems. There are several variegated cultivars, of which the best known is *D. reflexa* 'Song of India', with white- or cream-edged leaves. Because pleomele is tolerant of many indoor environments, it is often seen in commercial interiors. Keep it away from drafts and cold air.
Light: Provide at least moderate light but no direct sunlight.

Water: Let plant approach dryness before watering, then water thoroughly and discard drainage.
Humidity: Average indoor humidity levels.
Temperatures: 65° to 70° F at night, 75° to 80° F during the day.
Fertilization: Fertilize lightly throughout the growing season.
Propagation: Take stem cuttings at any time, or start new plants by air layering.
Grooming: Pick off yellowed leaves. Trim brown leaf tips.
Repotting: Repot infrequently.
Problems: Leaves will drop if soil is too wet or too dry.

Dracaena sanderana
Ribbon-plant, sander's dracaena

Ribbon-plant will get tall in time, but it is usually sold as a small plant less than a foot tall. The leathery, narrow leaves have white stripes along the edges. It does well in a dish garden, terrarium, or dimly lit spot. If the plant gets too leggy or spindly, air-layer it and replant. Water and fertilize lightly if the plant is in low light. Keep it out of drafts to avoid leaf scorch.
Light: Will survive in low (reading-level) light.
Water: Let plant approach dryness before watering, then water thoroughly and discard drainage.
Humidity: Average indoor humidity levels.
Temperatures: 55° to 60° F at night, 70° to 75° F during the day.
Fertilization: Fertilize lightly throughout the growing season.
Propagation: Take stem cuttings at any time, or start new plants by air layering.
Grooming: Pick off yellowed leaves.
Repotting: Repot infrequently.
Problems: Leaves will scorch if plant is in a draft or dry air.

Dracaena surculosa
Golddust dracaena

The form of golddust dracaena and the shape of its leaves make it different from other dracaenas. Golddust dracaena is small and shrubby. It has fairly broad leaves, somewhat like those of an elm tree. They are brilliantly spotted with yellow or cream markings. Several cultivars, such as 'Florida Beauty', are now available that are even more colorful than the species. Golddust dracaena must have good light and be kept constantly moist. It is slow growing and will rarely reach more than 2 feet tall, even in ample light.

Light: Place in a bright, indirectly lit south, east, or west window.

Water: Keep evenly moist. Water thoroughly and discard drainage.

Humidity: Average indoor humidity levels.

Temperatures: 55° to 60° F at night, 70° to 75° F during the day.

Fertilization: Fertilize lightly throughout the growing season.

Propagation: Take stem cuttings at any time.

Grooming: Keep to desired height and shape with light pruning or clipping at any time.

Repotting: Repot in winter or early spring as needed.

Problems: Leaves will scorch if plant is in a draft or dry air and will drop if soil is too wet or too dry.

Epipremnum aureum
Epipremnum, pothos, devil's-ivy

Epipremnum (also known as *Scindapsus*) is commonly used in commercial interiors as a vining ground cover or as a cascading accent plant, often in a hanging basket. Its heart-shaped, leathery leaves look somewhat like the heart-leaf philodendron's. The species is irregularly marbled yellow, with better color in good light. *E. aureum* 'Marble Queen' is more heavily mottled with white and gray-green. Pinch back stem tips occasionally to promote branching. Cut back old runners or vines when they get leggy or loop them over the pot and root them near their ends.

Light: Provide at least moderate light but no direct sunlight.

Water: Keep evenly moist. Water thoroughly and discard drainage.

Humidity: Average indoor humidity levels.

Temperatures: 50° to 55° F at night, 60° to 65° F during the day.

Fertilization: Fertilize lightly throughout the growing season.

Propagation: Take stem cuttings at any time.

Grooming: Pick off yellowed leaves. Keep to desired height and shape by pinching back stem tips or with light pruning or clipping at any time.

Repotting: Repot at any time.

Problems: Poor drainage, too-frequent watering, or standing in water will cause root rot. Will get spindly and weak if light is too low.

Eriobotrya japonica
Japanese loquat

Japanese loquat is a small tree or shrub often used in southwestern landscapes as an informal hedge or an espaliered specimen plant. The 6- to 12-inch-long leaves are dark green on top and tan beneath. Clusters of small, fragrant, white flowers open in late fall or early winter. If given enough light, fertilizer, and warmth, small edible fruit will ripen in mid- to late spring. Loquats will grow well in a solarium or greenhouse. They can get quite large; prune them well in spring to maintain a comfortable size and proper shape.

Light: Provide 4 hours or more of direct sunlight from a south window. Does best in a greenhouse setting.

Water: Keep evenly moist. Water thoroughly and discard drainage.

Humidity: Average indoor humidity levels.

Temperatures: 55° to 60° F at night, 70° to 75° F during the day.

Fertilization: Use an acid-based fertilizer and add trace elements once in spring.

Propagation: Take cuttings from stems or shoots before they have hardened or matured.

Grooming: Prune in early spring, being careful not to cut off flower buds or young fruit.

Repotting: Repot infrequently.

Problems: Will not bloom if light is too low. If soil is too wet or too dry, leaves will drop.

Euonymus fortunei
Winter creeper

Winter creeper is often used outdoors in northern states as a semievergreen climbing plant. Indoors, it does best in a cool location, such as an entranceway. The trailing stems will climb and attach themselves to vertical surfaces, so it is best to train the plant onto a wall or post. The variegated form of this slow-growing plant, *E. fortunei* 'Aureo-variegata', is particularly popular.

Dracaena surculosa 'Florida Beauty'

Epipremnum aureum

Eriobotrya japonica

Euonymus fortunei 'Ivory Jade'

Euonymus japonica

× *Fatshedera lizei*

Indoors, it will grow to 2 feet or more. The all-green varieties are rarely grown indoors.

Light: Place in a bright, indirectly lit south, east, or west window.

Water: Keep evenly moist. Water thoroughly and discard drainage.

Humidity: Average indoor humidity levels.

Temperatures: 40° to 45° F at night, 60° to 65° F during the day.

Fertilization: Fertilize lightly throughout the growing season.

Propagation: Take cuttings from stems or shoots before they have hardened or matured.

Grooming: Keep to desired height and shape with light pruning or clipping at any time.

Repotting: Repot infrequently.

Problems: Subject to infestations of scale and mealybug.

Euonymus japonica
Evergreen euonymus

Many evergreen euonymus cultivars are used outdoors as semievergreen foundation plantings. Indoors, the woody, bushy plants do well if given ample light. The foliage is about ½ inch long, produced abundantly all along the stems and often variegated. Popular cultivars for indoor use include *E. japonica* 'Aureo-variegata', 'Microphyllus Variegatus', and 'Silver Queen'. Keep these plants constantly moist and do not allow them to become pot bound. Stress may make them susceptible to spider mites.

Light: Provide at least 4 hours of curtain-filtered sunlight from a bright south, east, or west window.

Water: Keep evenly moist. Water thoroughly and discard drainage.

Humidity: Average indoor humidity levels.

Temperatures: 40° to 45° F at night, 60° to 65° F during the day.

Fertilization: Fertilize lightly throughout the growing season.

Propagation: Take cuttings from stems or shoots before they have hardened or matured.

Grooming: Keep to desired height and shape with light pruning or clipping at any time.

Repotting: Repot infrequently.

Problems: Spider mites can be a problem, especially if air is too dry. Subject to crown rot in overly moist

conditions. Leaves will drop if soil is too wet or too dry.

× Fatshedera lizei
Tree-ivy, aralia-ivy

Tree-ivy is a hybrid, a cross between English ivy and Japanese aralia. It is semierect, with a green, partially woody stem and leaves that are sometimes 10 inches across. Tree-ivy usually needs staking to keep it upright. The variegated cultivar, *F. lizei* 'Variegata', is particularly popular for indoor culture.

Light: In winter, keep in about 4 hours of direct sunlight. In summer, provide curtain-filtered sunlight from a south or west window.

Water: Keep evenly moist. Water thoroughly and discard drainage.

Humidity: Requires moist air. Use a humidifier for best results.

Temperatures: 40° to 45° F at night, 60° to 65° F during the day.

Fertilization: Fertilize lightly throughout the growing season.

Propagation: Take stem cuttings at any time, or start new plants by air layering.

Grooming: Prune in early spring. Give plant plenty of room.

Repotting: Repot in winter or early spring as needed.

Problems: Leaves will drop if soil is too wet or too dry.

Fatsia japonica
Japanese aralia

Japanese aralia is a handsome, evergreen plant with bold, lobed leaves of shiny green, occasionally variegated with white. In frost-free climates it can be grown outdoors, but it also makes an excellent contribution to indoor gardens. It's fast growing, durable, and tolerant of many environments. It is particularly easy to grow in a cool, well-ventilated location with bright light. Wash and mist the leaves regularly and feed every 2 weeks during the growing season, otherwise the leaves may yellow from lack of nitrogen. The plant needs to rest during winter, so move it to a cool spot and water much less frequently than usual. Remove any flower buds that emerge on the mature plant to prevent it from diverting its energies to reproduction. If it begins to look gangly or has misshapen leaves, trim it back to the stalk.

Light: Place in a bright, indirectly lit south, east, or west window.
Water: Keep evenly moist. Water thoroughly and discard drainage. In winter, keep almost dry, watering infrequently.
Humidity: Average indoor humidity levels.
Temperatures: 50° to 55° F at night, 60° to 65° F during the day.
Fertilization: Fertilize lightly throughout the growing season.
Propagation: Take cuttings from recently matured stems or shoots.
Grooming: Keep to desired height and shape with light pruning or clipping at any time.
Repotting: Repot infrequently, in winter or early spring when needed.
Problems: Poor drainage, too-frequent watering, or standing in water will cause root rot.

Ferns

Ferns, with the delicate composition of their spore-producing fronds, instill a room with a peaceful air. Ferns are among the oldest plants on earth; only the algae and the mosses are older. They come in a multitude of shapes and sizes, such as the small ribbon fern, with its ribbonlike fronds, or the large maidenhair fern, which has fan-shaped leaflets. Several types grouped together in entryways, patios, or conservatories can create a stunning design. They also work well displayed alone, in pots, or in hanging baskets.

The secret of success in growing ferns lies in your ability to match as nearly as possible their natural environment. The better you can imitate the moist, cool air and light shade of a tropical forest, the better your fern will grow. Since its natural habitat has only dappled light, avoid exposing your plant to the direct sunlight that strikes a windowsill. Hot, dry air is a problem for ferns. Both the air and the soil must always be moist. Provide humidity by placing the pot on a humidifying tray or in a larger pot of moist peat moss. Most ferns will grow well in average indoor temperatures during the day, with a drop in temperature at night.

The variety of ferns is enormous. Of the two thousand or so species to choose from, the following are some of the most popular types to grow indoors.

Adiantum
Maidenhair fern

Maidenhair ferns are found in northern states growing in damp, cool spots near mountain streams. Their fronds have striking black stems and leaflets that are broad but frilled. The leaflets tend to be borne horizontally and seem suspended in midair on a mature plant. Their main limitation indoors is that they require an extremely damp atmosphere. A lighted terrarium is ideal for growing maidenhair ferns. Give them plenty of room so they can mature properly. Common varieties include *A. hispidulum, A. raddianum,* and *A. tenerum.*
Light: Provide at least moderate light but no direct sunlight.
Water: Keep plant very moist, but do not allow to stand in water.
Humidity: Requires moist air. Use a humidifier for best results. Does best in a terrarium.
Temperatures: 50° to 55° F at night, 60° to 65° F during the day.
Fertilization: Fertilize lightly.
Propagation: Start new plants by dividing an old specimen.
Grooming: Cut back in early spring.
Repotting: Repot in winter or early spring, as needed.
Problems: Dry soil or a high level of soluble salts may damage roots, causing plant to die back. Leaves will scorch if plant is in a draft or dry air.

Asplenium bulbiferum
Mother fern

The mother fern has fronds that arch outward from the crown, like those of its cousin the bird's-nest fern. They are finely divided into extremely narrow leaflets and carry tiny plantlets that can be used for propagation, hence the common name of mother fern. *A. daucifolium* is similar in appearance, but more delicate.
Light: Provide at least moderate light but no direct sunlight.
Water: Keep evenly moist. Water thoroughly and discard drainage.
Humidity: Requires moist air. Use a humidifier for best results.
Temperatures: 50° to 55° F at night, 60° to 65° F during the day.
Fertilization: Fertilize twice a year, in early spring and midsummer.
Propagation: Remove plantlets or rooted side shoots as they form.

Fatsia japonica

Fern: *Adiantum*

Fern: *Asplenium bulbiferum*

Fern: *Asplenium nidus*

Fern: *Blechnum occidentale*

Grooming: Pick off yellowed fronds.
Repotting: Repot in winter or early spring, as needed.
Problems: Leaves will scorch if plant is in a draft or dry air.

Asplenium nidus
Bird's-nest fern, spleenwort

Bird's-nest fern will grow into a large plant in time. The graceful, arching fronds can reach 15 inches. They emerge from a dark crown that looks like a bird's nest. The plant is relatively easy to grow indoors, but be sure to give it plenty of room.
Light: Will survive in low (reading-level) light.
Water: Let plant approach dryness before watering, then water thoroughly and discard drainage.
Humidity: Average indoor humidity levels.
Temperatures: 48° to 45° F at night, 60° to 65° F during the day.
Fertilization: Fertilize lightly.
Propagation: Brush spores onto a clay pot and cover with a plastic bag to maintain dampness. Keep out of direct sunlight.
Grooming: Pick off yellowed fronds.
Repotting: Transplant young plants when they are large enough to put into soil. Repot mature plants in winter or early spring, as needed.
Problems: Leaves will scorch if plant is in a draft or dry air.

Blechnum gibbum

When young, blechnum forms a neat, ground-hugging rosette of deeply lobed fronds, reaching a diameter of 3 feet. As it ages, it forms a narrow, black trunk up to 3 feet tall. As one of the easiest tree ferns to grow, and also one of the least massive, it is ideal for homes and apartments. It is unfortunately rarely available in its adult form. Buy it as a young plant . . . and be patient!
Light: Place in a bright, indirectly lit south, east, or west window.
Water: Keep very moist at all times, but do not allow to stand in water.
Humidity: Requires moist air. Use a humidifier for best results.
Temperatures: 60° to 65° F at night, 75° to 80° F during the day.
Fertilization: Fertilize lightly throughout the growing season.

Propagation: Root the occasional offsets or grow from spores.
Grooming: Pick off yellowed fronds.
Repotting: Repot infrequently.
Problems: Leaves will scorch if plant is in a draft or dry air.

Cibotium chamissoi
Hawaiian tree fern, Mexican tree fern

Hawaiian tree ferns are suited only for spacious locations. They are magnificent plants in an indoor solarium, beside an indoor pool, or in a greenhouse. The fronds are finely divided and up to 6 feet long. The plants can be purchased with a trunk several feet high if desired. A related fern, *C. schiedei* (Mexican tree fern), usually has a "trunk" only a few inches high or no trunk at all.
Light: Provide at least 4 hours of curtain-filtered sunlight from a bright south, east, or west window.
Water: Keep evenly moist. Water thoroughly and discard drainage.
Humidity: Requires moist air. Use a humidifier for best results.
Temperatures: 55° to 60° F at night, 70° to 75° F during the day.
Fertilization: Fertilize lightly.
Propagation: Propagation is difficult but can be done from spores.
Grooming: Pick off yellowed fronds.
Repotting: Repot in winter or early spring, as needed.
Problems: Leaves will scorch if plant is in a draft or dry air.

Cyathea
Tree fern

Tree ferns become truly tree size outdoors in tropical environments. Indoors, they grow slowly, so they can make fine specimen plants for many years in a spacious area. The finely divided fronds, which emerge from the top of a 3- or 4-foot-high trunk, may reach 2 feet in length. Purchase a fairly large plant so that you can enjoy its tree stature without having to wait 10 years. Keep the soil wet. Place in a humid spot protected from drafts.
Light: Place in a bright, indirectly lit south, east, or west window.
Water: Keep very moist at all times, but do not allow to stand in water.
Humidity: Requires moist air. Use a humidifier for best results.
Temperatures: 50° to 55° F at night, 65° to 70° F during the day.

Fertilization: Fertilize lightly.
Propagation: Not generally attempted but can be done from spores.
Grooming: Pick off yellowed fronds.
Repotting: Repot infrequently, in winter or early spring when needed.
Problems: Leaves will scorch if plant is in a draft or dry air.

Cyrtomium falcatum
Holly fern

Of all the ferns, holly fern is perhaps the most tolerant of indoor environments. It is a slow-growing plant that may grow to 2 feet in time. The fronds are divided into fairly large leaflets 3 to 5 inches long and up to 1 or 2 inches wide. Like holly leaves, they are a glistening green. The cultivar 'Rochfordianum' is the most commonly grown holly fern.
Light: Will survive in low (reading-level) light.
Water: Keep evenly moist. Water thoroughly and discard drainage.
Humidity: Requires moist air. Use a humidifier for best results.
Temperatures: 40° to 45° F at night, 60° to 65° F during the day.
Fertilization: Fertilize lightly.
Propagation: Start new plants by dividing an old specimen.
Grooming: Pick off yellowed fronds.
Repotting: Repot in winter or early spring, as needed.
Problems: Leaves will scorch if plant is in a draft or dry air. Subject to crown rot in overly moist conditions.

Davallia
Deer's-foot fern, rabbit's-foot fern, squirrel's-foot fern

Like the polypody fern, ferns in the *Davallia* genus are noted for their furry rhizomes, which creep over and down the sides of the growing container and resemble animal feet. The plants become more interesting with age, so do not divide them often. They are attractive in a hanging basket; the "feet" cascade or creep downward. The fronds are usually finely divided and delicate. The most commonly available species include *D. mariesii*, *D. fejeensis* 'Plumosa', and *D. trichomanoides*.
Light: Provide at least moderate light but no direct sunlight.
Water: Keep evenly moist. Water thoroughly and discard drainage.

Fern: *Blechnum gibbum*

Fern: *Cyathea*

Fern: *Davallia mariesii*

Fern: *Cyrtomium falcatum*

Fern: *Nephrolepis exaltata* 'Bostoniensis'

Fern: *Pellaea rotundifolia*

Fern: *Platycerium bifurcatum*

Humidity: Requires moist air. Use a humidifier for best results.
Temperatures: 50° to 55° F at night, 65° to 70° F during the day.
Fertilization: Fertilize lightly throughout the growing season.
Propagation: Start new plants by dividing an old specimen.
Grooming: Pick off yellowed fronds.
Repotting: Repot infrequently.
Problems: Leaves will scorch if plant is in a draft or dry air.

Nephrolepis exaltata 'Bostoniensis'
Boston fern, sword fern, Dallas fern

Boston ferns are the most popular indoor ferns for good reason: They are striking and they tolerate a variety of indoor conditions. Their arching form makes them useful for hanging baskets. Many new cultivars are available. Some have particularly long fronds; others, such as 'Fluffy Ruffles', are small plants with more finely divided fronds than the older cultivars. *N. exaltata* 'Dallasii' (Dallas fern) is a particularly choice cultivar because of its ability to adapt to dry air. The similar *N. obliterata* 'Kimberley Queen' is a close relative of the Boston fern and is likewise especially tolerant of dry air. If plants begin to thin out and weaken, repot them and place them in better light.
Light: Provide at least moderate light but no direct sunlight.
Water: Let plant approach dryness before watering, then water thoroughly and discard drainage.
Humidity: Average indoor humidity levels.
Temperatures: 50° to 55° F at night, 65° to 70° F during the day.
Fertilization: Fertilize all year, more heavily in summer.
Propagation: Start new plants by dividing an old specimen, or root the tips of the runners.
Grooming: Pick off yellowed fronds. Keep to desired height and shape with light pruning or clipping at any time.
Repotting: Repot infrequently.
Problems: Poor drainage, too-frequent watering, or standing in water will cause root rot. Leaves will drop if plant is suddenly moved into low light. Plant will get spindly and weak if light is too low.

Pellaea rotundifolia
Button fern

The round, shiny leaflets of the button fern are borne on ground-hugging black stems, making the plant look more like a ground cover than a fern. Often sold in a small hanging basket, it is also a fine choice for terrariums and plant shelves.
Light: Place in a bright, indirectly lit south, east, or west window.
Water: Keep very moist at all times, but do not allow to stand in water.
Humidity: Requires moist air. Use a humidifier for best results.
Temperatures: 55° to 60° F at night, 70° to 75° F during the day.
Fertilization: Fertilize lightly throughout the growing season.
Propagation: Divide in spring, or grow from spores.
Grooming: Pick off yellowed fronds.
Repotting: Repot infrequently.
Problems: Leaves will scorch if plant is in a draft or dry air.

Platycerium bifurcatum
Staghorn fern

Staghorn ferns are epiphytes and grow on surfaces rather than in soil or potting media. They can be purchased on bark slabs, clumps of sphagnum moss, or cork boards. Growth is slow, but eventually they develop massive fronds that resemble the antlers of a large animal. A wall in a humid, brightly lit location is an ideal spot for hanging staghorn ferns. Plantlets will eventually form at the base of the parent plant and emerge between the large, flat basal fronds. Water staghorn ferns by attaching some moisture-holding material, such as sphagnum moss, to the growing surface at the base of the plant. Once a week take the plant down and soak it in a pail or sink.
Light: Provide at least 4 hours of curtain-filtered sunlight from a bright south, east, or west window.
Water: Keep evenly moist. Water thoroughly and discard drainage.
Humidity: Requires moist air. Use a humidifier for best results.
Temperatures: 50° to 55° F at night, 65° to 70° F during the day.
Fertilization: Fertilize lightly.
Propagation: Remove plantlets or rooted side shoots as they form.
Grooming: Pick off yellowed fronds.

Repotting: Replace or replenish the water-holding sphagnum when needed.
Problems: Leaves will scorch if plant is in a draft or dry air.

Polypodium
Bear's-paw fern, hare's-foot fern, golden polypody fern

Polypodium gained its common names from the furry rhizomes that grow along the surface of the soil and resemble animal feet. The rhizomes eventually creep over the sides of the pot. The tough fronds are divided into a few large lobes. As with most ferns, coolness, light fertilization, and infrequent repotting are best. Many indoor gardeners grow this fern on a bark slab, but they usually keep it in a terrarium, where high humidity can be maintained. The most popular cultivar is *P. aureum* 'Mandaianum'. All are easy to grow.
Light: Provide at least 4 hours of curtain-filtered sunlight from a bright south, east, or west window.
Water: Let plant approach dryness before watering, then water thoroughly and discard drainage.
Humidity: Average indoor humidity levels.
Temperatures: 50° to 55° F at night, 60° to 65° F during the day.
Fertilization: Fertilize lightly.
Propagation: Start new plants by dividing an old specimen.
Grooming: Pick off yellowed fronds.
Repotting: Repot infrequently.
Problems: Leaves will scorch if plant is in a draft or dry air; leaves will drop if plant is suddenly moved into low light.

Polystichum tsus-simense
Dwarf leatherleaf fern

Dwarf leatherleaf fern is a slow-growing plant ideally suited to terrariums and dish gardens. When it grows too large for those spaces, transfer it to a hanging basket or individual pot. The shiny, deep green fronds are deeply cut and quite tolerant of dry air.
Light: Provide at least moderate light but no direct sunlight.
Water: Let plant approach dryness before watering, then water thoroughly and discard drainage.
Humidity: Requires moist air. Use a humidifier for best results.
Temperatures: 50° to 55° F at night, 60° to 65° F during the day.

Fertilization: Fertilize lightly.
Propagation: Start new plants by dividing an old specimen.
Grooming: Pick off yellowed fronds.
Repotting: Repot in late spring, if needed.
Problems: Leaves will drop if soil is too wet or too dry. Dry soil or a high level of soluble salts may damage roots, causing plant to die back.

Pteris
Table fern, brake fern, fan table fern, silverleaf fern

Table ferns are so named because they grow slowly indoors, remaining small and useful as a table centerpiece. The fronds are variously divided and variegated. *P. cretica* 'Albo-lineata' (variegated table fern), for example, bears a broad band of creamy white down each slightly wavy leaflet and the *P. ensiformis* 'Victoriae' (silverleaf fern) has finely divided fronds with a silver band down the middle. *P. cretica* 'Wilsonii' (fan table fern) has bright green, fan-shaped fronds with dense crests at the tips. There are many other choice varieties. Despite their name, do not keep these ferns permanently on a table in dim light. They require a little more humidity than is generally available indoors.
Light: Provide at least moderate light but no direct sunlight.
Water: Keep evenly moist. Water thoroughly and discard drainage.
Humidity: Requires moist air. Use a humidifier for best results.
Temperatures: 50° to 55° F at night, 60° to 65° F during the day.
Fertilization: Fertilize lightly throughout the growing season.
Propagation: Start new plants by dividing an old specimen.
Grooming: Pick off yellowed fronds.
Repotting: Repot at any time.
Problems: Leaves will scorch if plant is in a draft or dry air.

Sphaeropteris cooperi
Tree fern

Tree ferns are best suited for a solarium, indoor swimming pool area, or similar large indoor setting. The fronds are several feet long and have hairy stems. They generally grow from a crown at the end of a long trunk. Plants of this size are quite old, but can be purchased from a specialty store (they may still be sold under their old name, *Alsophila*).

Fern: *Polypodium aureum*

Fern: *Polystichum tsus-simense*

Fern: *Pteris cretica*

Ficus benjamina

Ficus deltoidea

Ficus elastica 'Variegata'

Keep the soil moist and the air humid and warm.

Light: Place in a bright, indirectly lit south, east, or west window.
Water: Keep very moist at all times, but do not allow to stand in water.
Humidity: Requires moist air. Use a humidifier for best results.
Temperatures: 65° to 70° F at night, 75° to 80° F during the day.
Fertilization: Fertilize lightly.
Propagation: Not generally attempted but can be done from spores.
Grooming: Pick off yellowed fronds.
Repotting: Repot infrequently.
Problems: Leaves will scorch if plant is in a draft or dry air.

Ficus
Fig

Fig is a large, diverse family of more than 800 tropical trees, shrubs, and vines. It includes not only *F. carica* (edible fig), but a number of ornamental plants for container gardening. Listed below are some indoor favorites.

Figs will do well if they have good light, rich soil kept evenly moist, and frequent feeding. Guard against overwatering, and protect against cold drafts, dry heat, and any sudden changes in environment.

Shrubby Figs

Some ficus naturally form compact shrubs. They normally don't become much larger than 3 or 4 feet in height and can be kept considerably smaller by judicious pruning.

Ficus deltoidea
Mistletoe fig

The mistletoe fig (also known as *F. diversifolia*) is an interesting indoor shrub. It bears spreading branches covered with small, rounded to wedge-shaped leaves and many tiny (but inedible) green figs that turn red in bright sun.

Ficus 'Green Island'
Green Island fig

A fig of purportedly hybrid origin, Green Island fig has thick branches that bear leaves resembling those of *F. benjamina* but less pointed and much

thicker. Although it is slow growing, it is particularly easy to grow.

Ficus triangularis
Triangleleaf fig

Triangleleaf fig resembles a large mistletoe fig, but it has larger leaves that have a distinctly triangular outline and rounded edges. Like the mistletoe fig, it produces numerous, tiny, but inedible, figs.

Tree-Sized Figs

The following figs are normally sold as indoor trees, from 3 to 8 feet or more in height. Some are sold with braided trunks, giving them extra support. The smaller-leaved varieties can be pruned and grown as indoor shrubs.

Ficus benjamina
Weeping fig

Ficus benjamina holds a prominent position among container plants because it is favored by so many designers. It has pale brown bark like birch bark and graceful, arching branches loaded with glossy, pointed leaves. It grows from 2 to 18 feet tall. Several variegated forms, with leaves speckled or splotched in white or yellow, are also available. This plant often loses most of its leaves when moved to a new location. It will need a period of adjustment, but with care it will flourish again.

Ficus elastica
Rubber plant

Ficus elastica and the larger-leaved *F. elastica* 'Decora' are old favorites commonly known as rubber plants. They have bold, deep green leaves on stems 2 to 10 feet tall. 'Variegata' has long, narrow leaves that make rippling patterns of grass green, metallic gray, and creamy yellow. When a rubber plant becomes too lanky, cut off the top and select a side branch to form a new main shoot, or air-layer the plant.

Ficus lyrata
Fiddleleaf fig

Ficus lyrata (also known as *F. pandurata*) is a striking container plant. It has durable, papery leaves of deep green in a fiddle shape. The plant grows 5 to 10 feet tall.

Ficus maclellandii 'Alii'

This fig is a recent introduction with long, narrow, pointed leaves, which give it a bamboo appearance. It makes a striking specimen plant and is more tolerant of being moved than *F. benjamina*.

Ficus retusa
Indian-laurel

Indian-laurel, often listed as *F. retusa nitida,* is one of the easiest evergreen trees to grow indoors. It is similar to *F. benjamina* (weeping fig), but has a slightly larger leaf and is more upright in its branching habit. Indian-laurels are commonly seen in commercial interiors. Grow as a single-stemmed shrub when it is small. As it grows, gradually prune it into a tree form.

Ficus stricta

Ficus stricta is similar to *F. benjamina,* but has larger, less pointed leaves. It is often listed as *F. benjamina* var. *nuda.*

Care of Tree-Sized and Shrubby Ficus

Light: Provide 3 to 4 hours of curtain-filtered sunlight from a bright south, east, or west window.
Water: Let plant approach dryness before watering, then water thoroughly and discard drainage.
Humidity: Average indoor humidity levels.
Temperatures: 50° to 55° F at night, 65° to 70° F during the day.
Fertilization: Fertilize all year, more heavily in summer.
Propagation: Take stem cuttings before they have hardened or matured or air-layer.
Grooming: Prune to desired form as plant matures.
Repotting: Repot infrequently.
Problems: Dry soil or a high level of soluble salts may damage roots, causing plant to die back. Leaves will drop if plant is suddenly moved into low light.

Climbing Figs

In outdoor settings climbing figs scale great heights into treetops and up walls and cliff faces. Indoors, unless they are in a humid greenhouse, they rarely produce the clinging aerial roots that would allow them to climb. However, they can be trained up trellises, used as ground covers, or grown as hanging plants. Their thin leaves are more sensitive to dry air than those of other figs.

Ficus pumila
Creeping fig

Creeping fig has tiny, heart-shaped leaves. It's a fast-growing trailer that looks especially attractive in a hanging basket or cascading from a shelf. It also makes an excellent ground cover for terrariums. Variegated and oakleaf versions are available. Variegated cultivars sometimes produce all-green branches, which should be removed.

Ficus sagittata 'Variegata'
Variegated rooting fig

Also sold as *F. radicans* 'Variegata', variegated rooting fig bears thin, pointed, 2- to 4-inch leaves heavily marked with creamy white. It makes an elegant hanging-basket plant. Brown patches in the variegated areas are due to too much cold or sun.

Care of Climbing Figs

Light: Place in a bright, indirectly lit south, east, or west window.
Water: Keep evenly moist. Water thoroughly and discard drainage.
Humidity: Require moist air. Use a humidifier for best results.
Temperatures: 60° to 65° F at night, 70° to 75° F during the day.
Fertilization: Fertilize only during late spring and summer.
Propagation: Take stem cuttings at any time.
Grooming: Pick off yellowed leaves. Pinch or prune plant regularly for a fuller shape.
Repotting: Repot infrequently.
Problems: Leaves will scorch if plants are in a draft or dry air.

Fittonia
Fittonia, nerveplant, mosaic-plant

The intricately veined, oval leaves of fittonia grow semiupright, then trail over the sides of the container.

Ficus lyrata

Ficus maclellandii 'Alii'

Ficus pumila

Fittonia verschaffeltii var. argyroneura

Gynura aurantiaca

Hedera canariensis

F. verschaffeltii var. *argyroneura* displays a mosaic pattern of white veins; *F. verschaffeltii* var. *argyroneura* 'Minima' bears small leaves. *F. verschaffeltii* var. *verschaffeltii* has deep red veins on paper-thin, olive green leaves. They all make striking hanging plants, and the small types work well in terrariums. Fittonias will thrive in most households.

Light: Provide at least moderate light but no direct sunlight from a north or east window.

Water: Water thoroughly, but allow to dry between waterings. Water lightly during winter.

Humidity: Requires moist air. Use a humidifier for best results.

Temperatures: 65° to 70° F at night, 75° to 80° F during the day. Move to a cool spot during the winter.

Fertilization: Fertilize lightly throughout the growing season.

Propagation: Take cuttings from recently matured stems or shoots.

Grooming: Keep to desired height and shape with light pruning or clipping at any time. As older plants become unattractive, start them over from cuttings.

Repotting: Repot in winter or early spring, as needed.

Problems: Subject to crown rot in overly moist conditions. Will get spindly and weak if light is too low.

Geogenanthus undatus
Seersucker-plant

On its short stems the seersucker-plant produces 2-inch leaves that have white stripes and a puckered texture. It will remain small. The plant grows well indoors if given warmth at night.

Light: Provide at least 4 hours of curtain-filtered sunlight from a bright south, east, or west window.

Water: Keep evenly moist. Water thoroughly and discard drainage.

Humidity: Requires moist air. Use a humidifier for best results.

Temperatures: 65° to 70° F at night, 75° to 80° F during the day.

Fertilization: Fertilize all year, more heavily in summer.

Propagation: Take stem cuttings at any time.

Grooming: Pick off yellowed leaves. As older plants become unattractive, start them over from cuttings.

Repotting: Repot at any time.

Problems: Leaves will scorch if plant is in a draft or dry air.

Gynura aurantiaca
Velvetplant, purple passionplant

A trailing plant, velvetplant has intensely purple leaves and stems with thick, reddish hairs covering all surfaces. It is easy to grow, and, if pruned, is attractive in a hanging basket. With enough light, the plant will produce clusters of tiny flowers with white petals and yellow centers. It is best to pick these off quickly, however, because they have an unpleasant aroma and will produce a mess of dropping petals and seedpods. The plant probably won't flower if it is grown in low light.

Light: Place in a bright, indirectly lit south, east, or west window.

Water: Keep evenly moist. Water thoroughly and discard drainage.

Humidity: Average indoor humidity levels.

Temperatures: 55° to 60° F at night, 70° to 75° F during the day.

Fertilization: Fertilize lightly throughout the growing season.

Propagation: Take stem cuttings at any time.

Grooming: Keep to desired height and shape with light pruning or clipping at any time.

Repotting: Repot at any time.

Problems: Dry soil or a high level of soluble salts may damage roots, causing plant to die back. Subject to infestations of whiteflies and aphids.

Hedera canariensis
Canary Island ivy, Algerian ivy

Canary Island ivy is a fast-growing plant with large leaves. It can be grown in a basket or trained on a trellis. The most popular cultivar, *H. canariensis* 'Variegata' (also known as 'Gloire-de-Marengo'), has green leaves with white variegation. Keep these ivies moist and warm when growing them indoors.

Light: Provide at least 4 hours of curtain-filtered sunlight from a bright south, east, or west window.

Water: Keep evenly moist. Water thoroughly and discard drainage.

Humidity: Average indoor humidity levels.

Temperatures: 65° to 70° F at night, 75° to 80° F during the day.

Fertilization: Fertilize all year, more heavily in summer.
Propagation: Take stem cuttings at any time.
Grooming: Keep to desired height and shape with light pruning or clipping at any time.
Repotting: Repot at any time.
Problems: Will get spindly and weak if light is too low.

Hedera helix
English ivy

Many plants are called ivy, but the most famous is *H. helix*, the English ivy. Countless varieties of this trailing and climbing plant are available. 'Merion Beauty' has small leaves in the characteristic English ivy shape. 'Itsy Bitsy' is a tiny variety. Others have leaves that are curled, waved, or crinkled. 'Curlilocks' is an example. Still others have color variegation, such as the yellow-gold 'Gold Dust'; 'Glacier' is one of the white-variegated cultivars. Many ivies send out aerial roots that will climb rough surfaces—a brick fireplace wall, for example. You can also use them in large planters as a ground cover. They are excellent in hanging baskets and can be trained on a trellis.

Protected from hot, dry air, English ivy will flourish as long as a few basics are followed: Place it in a cool, bright location, and keep the soil and air moist. During the growing season, feed every 2 weeks. Bathe the foliage occasionally. Plants rest in both fall and winter.
Light: Place in a bright, indirectly lit south, east, or west window.
Water: Keep evenly moist. Water thoroughly and discard drainage.
Humidity: Average indoor humidity levels.
Temperatures: 40° to 45° F at night, 60° to 65° F during the day.
Fertilization: Fertilize lightly throughout the growing season.
Propagation: Take stem cuttings at any time.
Grooming: Keep to desired height and shape with light pruning or clipping at any time.
Repotting: Repot at any time.
Problems: Spider mites can be a problem, especially if air is too dry. Small leaves and elongated stems indicate lack of light. Brown leaf tips result from dry air. Green leaves on variegated types result from too little light.

Hemigraphis
Red-ivy, red-flame ivy

Red-ivy is a weak-stemmed plant with oval to heart-shaped leaves that are an attractive combination of metallic violet above and wine red underneath. Short-lived but inconspicuous white flowers appear in summer. There are two common varieties: *H. alternata* (also known as *H. colorata*), with small, truly heart-shaped leaves, and *H.* 'Exotica', with larger, puckered leaves.
Light: Provide at least moderate light but no direct sunlight.
Water: Water thoroughly, but allow to dry between waterings.
Humidity: Requires moist air. Use a humidifier for best results.
Temperatures: 65° to 70° F at night, 75° to 80° F during the day.
Fertilization: Fertilize lightly throughout the growing season.
Propagation: Take stem cuttings at any time.
Grooming: Keep to desired shape with light pruning or pinching at any time during the year.
Repotting: Repot in winter or early spring as needed.
Problems: Subject to crown rot in overly moist conditions. Will get spindly, weak, and pale if light is too low.

Heptapleurum arboricola
Dwarf or miniature schefflera

Although its common names may suggest a diminutive stature, *H. arboricola* is only smaller that its cousin, the common schefflera (*Brassaia actinophylla*) in leaf size; it can reach over 6 feet in height and diameter. Fortunately, unlike the common schefflera, it branches readily and can be kept in check through regular pruning. The compound leaves are up to 7 inches across and deep green. There are several named cultivars, including some with yellow variegation and notched leaves. All are easy to grow.
Light: Provide 3 to 4 hours of curtain-filtered sunlight from a bright south, east, or west window.
Water: Let plant approach dryness before watering, then water thoroughly and discard drainage.
Humidity: Average indoor humidity levels.
Temperatures: 50° to 55° F at night, 65° to 70° F during the day.

Hedera helix 'Kolibri'

Heptapleurum arboricola

Homalomena wallisii

Hypoestes phyllostachya

Iresine herbstii

Fertilization: Fertilize only during late spring and summer.
Propagation: Take stem cuttings at any time, or air-layer.
Grooming: Pick off yellowed leaves. Pinch or prune regularly to maintain a fuller shape.
Repotting: Repot infrequently.
Problems: Will get spindly and weak if light is too low. Leaves will drop if soil is too wet or too dry.

Homalomena
Homalomena

The decorative potential of homalomenas are only just being discovered. Some, such as *H. wallisii,* with its thick, oblong, dark green leaves mottled with yellow, are grown for their variegation. Others, such as *H.* 'King of Spades' and *H.* 'Queen of Hearts', are grown for their dark, shiny foliage.
Light: Place in a bright, indirectly lit south, east, or west window. Will survive in poor light but growth is minimal.
Water: Water thoroughly, but allow to dry between waterings.
Humidity: Requires moist air. Use a humidifier for best results.
Temperatures: 65° to 70° F at night, 75° to 80° F during the day.
Fertilization: Fertilize lightly throughout the growing season.
Propagation: Propagate from cuttings or by division.
Grooming: Pick off yellowed leaves.
Repotting: Repot infrequently.
Problems: Leaves may die back or dry up in dry air.

Hypoestes phyllostachya
Hypoestes, pink-polka-dot, freckle-face

The common names for *Hypoestes* come from the unusual pink spots on its leaves (its botanical name formerly was *H. sanguinolenta*). It's a bushy, herbaceous plant that grows rapidly in good light. Keep it well branched and to a height of 12 inches by pruning it frequently. Many colorful hybrids are now available, including 'Pink Splash' and red or white spotted cultivars.
Light: Provide at least 4 hours of curtain-filtered sunlight from a bright south, east, or west window.
Water: Let plant approach dryness before watering, then water thoroughly and discard drainage.

Humidity: Requires moist air. Use a humidifier for best results.
Temperatures: 65° to 70° F at night, 75° to 80° F during the day.
Fertilization: Fertilize lightly throughout the growing season.
Propagation: Grows easily from seed, which is readily available. Take stem cuttings at any time.
Grooming: Start new plants to replace old specimens when they get weak. Keep to desired height and shape with light pruning or clipping at any time.
Repotting: Repot in winter or early spring, as needed.
Problems: Will get spindly and weak if light is too low.

Iresine herbstii
Beefsteak-plant, bloodleaf

The ornamental foliage of this plant is an intense, full-bodied red, as its common name bloodleaf suggests. *I. herbstii* has heart-shaped leaves with light red veins. *I. herbstii* 'Aureo-reticulata' produces green leaves tinted with red and lined with yellow veins. These small plants make brilliant accents in groupings of larger plants.

They are easy to care for, but without a good deal of light, the leaves turn pale and the plant becomes leggy rather than bushy and compact. Water regularly and keep the air humid. In the summer, revive the plants with a vacation outdoors.
Light: Provide 4 hours or more of direct sunlight from a south window.
Water: Keep evenly moist. Water thoroughly and discard drainage.
Humidity: Requires moist air. Use a humidifier for best results.
Temperatures: 55° to 60° F at night, 70° to 75° F during the day.
Fertilization: Fertilize all year, more heavily in summer.
Propagation: Take cuttings from stems or shoots that have recently matured.
Grooming: Keep to desired height and shape with light pruning or clipping at any time.
Repotting: Repot in winter or early spring, as needed.
Problems: Will get spindly and weak if light is too low.

Laurus nobilis
Sweet bay, Grecian bay laurel

Sweet bay is seen in ancient artwork that depicts people wearing leafy crowns. The leaves are just as decorative today and are also used in cooking. As a houseplant sweet bay grows slowly, but eventually will become a 4-foot shrub. It prefers a well-lit, cool spot, such as an entranceway. Try to buy a large plant, since it will take several years to develop its bushy form.

Light: Provide 4 hours or more of direct sunlight from a south window.
Water: Let plant approach dryness before watering, then water thoroughly and discard drainage.
Humidity: Average indoor humidity levels.
Temperatures: 40° to 45° F at night, 60° to 65° F during the day.
Fertilization: Fertilize only during late spring and summer months.
Propagation: Take stem cuttings at any time.
Grooming: Keep to desired height and shape with light pruning or clipping at any time.
Repotting: Repot infrequently.
Problems: Poor drainage, too-frequent watering, or standing in water will cause root rot. Leaves will drop if soil is too wet or too dry.

Ledebouria socialis
Silver squill

Usually sold under its old name, *Scilla violacea*, silver squill is a small plant ideally suited for windowsills. It bears fleshy, pointed, olive green leaves splotched silvery gray with wine red undersides. The leaves are 2 to 4 inches long. The bulb grows above the soil and is purple in color. Clusters of tiny, green flowers are produced in spring but do not add much to the attractiveness of the plant.

Light: Provide at least 4 hours of curtain-filtered sunlight from a south, east, or west window.
Water: Water thoroughly, but allow to dry between waterings.
Humidity: Requires moist air. Use a humidifier for best results.
Temperatures: 55° to 60° F at night, 65° to 70° F during the day.
Fertilization: Fertilize lightly throughout the growing season.

Propagation: Pot bulblets that appear beside the parent bulb, or root plant after flowering.
Grooming: Pick off yellowed leaves and dried bulb tunics.
Repotting: Repot after flowering, setting the bulbs so that just the base is covered in potting mix.
Problems: Subject to crown rot if kept too moist. Will not bloom if light is too low.

Leea coccinea
West Indian holly

West Indian holly produces shiny, deep green compound leaves on an upright stem. Although it can reach 4 feet or more in height, it is generally kept pruned to 2 feet or less. There is also a purplish-leaved cultivar sold under the name *L. coccinea* 'Rubra'.

Light: Place in a bright, indirectly lit south, east, or west window.
Water: Water thoroughly, but allow to dry between waterings.
Humidity: Requires moist air. Use a humidifier for best results.
Temperatures: 65° to 70° F at night, 75° to 80° F during the day.
Fertilization: Fertilize lightly throughout the growing season.
Propagation: Take cuttings.
Grooming: Pick off faded leaves.
Repotting: Repot in winter or early spring, as needed.
Problems: Spots of black sap form on undersides of leaves. They are caused by a natural process called guttation and can be removed with a damp cloth.

Liriope
Liriope, lily-turf

Although well known in warmer parts of the country as a ground cover, lily-turf is only just beginning to be discovered as an attractive houseplant. It is grown for its graceful, grassy leaves and is popular in dish gardens and terrariums. Under very good conditions, it may bloom indoors, with clusters of dark blue to purple flowers. Dwarf and variegated cultivars, as well as those with dark, almost black leaves, are all suitable for indoor growing. The plants look fuller in a mass, so do not repot them often.

Light: Place in a bright, indirectly lit south, east, or west window.

Laurus nobilis

Ledebouria socialis

Liriope spicata 'Silver Dragon'

Maranta leuconeura var. erythroneura

Monstera deliciosa

Mimosa pudica

Water: Water thoroughly, but allow to dry between waterings. Water sparingly during the rest period.
Humidity: Average indoor humidity levels.
Temperatures: During the growing season, 65° to 70° F at night and 75° to 80° F during the day. During the winter rest period, 50° to 55° F at night, 65° to 70° F during the day.
Fertilization: Fertilize lightly throughout the growing season.
Propagation: Propagate from divisions in spring. Trim off brown leaf tips as necessary.
Grooming: Pick off yellowed leaves.
Repotting: Repot in spring as necessary.
Problems: Leaves may die back or dry up in dry air.

Maranta leuconeura
Prayer-plant

The name prayer-plant comes from the growth habit of *M. leuconeura* var. *kerchoviana.* In the daytime its satiny foliage lies flat, but at night the leaves turn upward, giving the appearance of praying hands. The plant reaches a height of about 8 inches. The two other main cultivars are *M. leuconeura* var. *leuconeura* and *M. leuconeura* var. *erythroneura.*

All three of these cultivars are fairly easy to grow. They grow best in a warm, humid environment with partial shade. Direct sunlight will cause the leaves to fade. Surround pots with peat moss or plant them in a grouping to improve humidity.
Light: Provide at least moderate light but no direct sunlight.
Water: Keep very moist during growth and flowering; at other times, allow to dry between waterings.
Humidity: Requires moist air. Use a humidifier for best results.
Temperatures: 55° to 60° F at night, 70° to 75° F during the day.
Fertilization: Fertilize lightly throughout the growing season.
Propagation: Start new plants by dividing an old specimen, or take stem cuttings at any time.
Grooming: Pick off yellowed leaves. Start new plants to replace old specimens when they get weak.
Repotting: Repot infrequently, in winter or early spring when needed.

Problems: Leaves will scorch if plant is in a draft or dry air. Poor drainage, too-frequent watering, or standing in water will cause root rot.

Mimosa pudica
Sensitive plant

When the finely divided leaflets of sensitive plant are touched, they immediately fold up. This habit makes the plant especially popular with children. It is a fast-growing plant easily started from seed. When the seedlings have several leaves, pinch back the stem tips to promote branching. Prune frequently to prevent legginess. Sensitive plant flowers readily, with small pink flowers. Keep it warm and in good light.
Light: Provide at least 4 hours of curtain-filtered sunlight from a bright south, east, or west window.
Water: Keep evenly moist. Water thoroughly and discard drainage.
Humidity: Average indoor humidity levels.
Temperatures: 65° to 70° F at night, 75° to 80° F during the day.
Fertilization: Fertilize lightly throughout the growing season.
Propagation: Start from seeds. Sow in a small pot and transplant seedlings as needed.
Grooming: Keep to desired height and shape with light pruning or clipping at any time. Prune seedlings only when several leaves have formed.
Repotting: Repot at any time.
Problems: Poor drainage, too-frequent watering, or standing in water will cause root rot. Will get spindly and weak if light is too low. Leaves will scorch if plant is in a draft or dry air. Plant will become unattractive with time, but can be started over with seeds at any season.

Monstera deliciosa
Monstera, split-leaf philodendron

Found in many homes, *Monstera deliciosa* climbs and sends out aerial roots that attach to supports or grow into the ground. Stems can reach 6 feet or more; they bear large, perforated, deeply cut leaves. *M. friedrichsthalii* is commonly available for use in hanging baskets. Its leaves are small, with wavy edges, and are perforated on either side of the midrib.

Monsteras are easy to grow as long as you provide a few essentials. Direct the aerial roots into the soil to give support to the weak stem. Keep soil barely moist in winter. Feed every 2 weeks during the growing season.

Light: Provide at least moderate light but no direct sunlight.

Water: During active growth water thoroughly, but allow to dry between waterings. Water sparingly in winter.

Humidity: Average indoor humidity levels.

Temperatures: 55° to 60° F at night, 70° to 75° F during the day.

Fertilization: Fertilize all year, more heavily in summer.

Propagation: Take stem cuttings or air-layer at any time.

Grooming: Wash mature leaves. Guide aerial roots into soil or onto a support. Cut tops of tall plants to limit their growth.

Repotting: Repot infrequently.

Problems: Waterlogged soil will cause leaves to weep around edges. Leaves with brown, brittle edges result from dry air. Brown edges and yellowed leaves are a symptom of overwatering or, less frequently, underfeeding. Dropping of lower leaves is normal. Serious leaf drop results from moving the plant or any other abrupt change. Young leaves often have no perforation. Low light may cause small, unperforated leaves to form.

Musa
Banana

The numerous plants in the genus *Musa* are all large, treelike, tropical plants best suited for greenhouses. Some species have attractive foliage and a semidwarf habit. Commercial container-plant growers are beginning to sell these smaller varieties, including the readily available *M. acuminata* 'Dwarf Cavendish', to florists, but even the smaller varieties grow large and need plenty of room. Banana plants require plenty of water and light. They are also very sensitive to cool temperatures at night. Do not expect them to flower and set fruit indoors unless they are in a greenhouse.

Light: Does best in a greenhouse setting.

Water: Keep very moist at all times, but do not allow to stand in water.

Humidity: Requires moist air. Use a humidifier for best results.

Temperatures: 65° to 70° F at night, 75° to 80° F during the day.

Fertilization: Fertilize all year, more heavily in summer.

Propagation: Take root cuttings at any time.

Grooming: Do not prune plant or cut it back. Give plenty of room.

Repotting: Repot at any time.

Problems: Leaves will scorch if plant is in a draft or dry air. Some species subject to spider mites in dry air.

Myrtus communis
True myrtle, Greek myrtle

True myrtle is commonly seen as a garden shrub in dry, warm climates; *M. communis* 'Microphylla', a small-leaved variety, is the most widely available. This cultivar is suitable for well-lit indoor gardens and is popular as an indoor bonsai specimen. It is a woody shrub that will grow 4 feet across if given enough room. The tiny leaves are aromatic and abundantly produced all along the stems. Myrtles have bright green leaves and attractive white flowers. Some cultivars have variegated foliage.

Light: In winter, keep in about 4 hours of direct sunlight. In summer, provide curtain-filtered sunlight from a south or west window.

Water: Let plant approach dryness before watering, then water thoroughly and discard drainage.

Humidity: Average indoor humidity levels.

Temperatures: 40° to 45° F at night, 60° to 65° F during the day.

Fertilization: Fertilize lightly throughout the growing season.

Propagation: Take cuttings from stems or shoots that have recently matured.

Grooming: Keep to desired height and shape with light pruning or clipping at any time.

Repotting: Repot in winter or early spring, as needed.

Problems: Spider mites can be a problem, especially if plant is too dry. Dry soil or a high level of soluble salts may damage roots, causing plant to die back. Leaves will scorch if plant is in a draft or dry air.

Musa ensete (Ensete ventricosum)

Myrtus communis 'Compacta'

Nandina domestica

Nicodemia diversifolia

Nandina domestica
Heavenly-bamboo

Heavenly-bamboo is a summer-flowering shrub, not a true bamboo. Indoors it needs plenty of sunlight and since it can grow to 8 feet, it is best suited for a greenhouse or solarium. It is also popular as a bonsai specimen. Keep heavenly-bamboo constantly wet and out of cold drafts.

Light: Provide 4 hours or more of direct sunlight from a south window. Does best in a greenhouse setting.

Water: Keep very moist at all times, but do not allow to stand in water.

Humidity: Requires moist air. Use a humidifier for best results.

Temperatures: 55° to 60° F at night, 70° to 75° F during the day.

Fertilization: Fertilize only when plant is growing actively.

Propagation: Start from seeds. Sow in a small pot and transplant seedlings as needed. Or divide a mature plant.

Grooming: Prune as needed.

Repotting: Prefers to be a little root bound. Cut back and repot as needed.

Problems: If plant is in a draft or dry air, leaves will scorch.

Nicodemia diversifolia
Nicodemia, indoor-oak

The true name for nicodemia is *Buddleia indica,* but it is never available under that name. A woody plant, it has small, shiny leaves shaped like those of an oak. With proper pruning, it will make an attractive indoor shrub about 1½ feet tall. Nicodemia grows slowly in summer and needs a moderate dormant period during winter. While it is resting, keep it warm, do not fertilize, and allow it to dry out between waterings.

Light: Provide at least 4 hours of curtain-filtered sunlight from a bright south, east, or west window.

Water: Let plant approach dryness before watering, then water thoroughly and discard drainage. Water less frequently during dormancy.

Humidity: Average indoor humidity levels.

Temperatures: 65° to 70° F at night, 75° to 80° F during the day.

Fertilization: Fertilize only when plant is growing actively.

Propagation: Take cuttings from stems or shoots before they have hardened or matured.

Grooming: Keep to desired height and shape with light pruning or clipping at any time. Prune in early spring.

Repotting: Repot in winter or early spring, as needed.

Problems: Dry soil or a high level of soluble salts may damage roots, causing plant to die back. Susceptible to spider mites.

Oplismenus hirtellus 'Variegatus'
Basketgrass

Basketgrass is one of the rare true grasses grown as a houseplant. The leaves are like those of lawn grasses but are striped green, white, and, in good light, pink. They hang down around the pot on long stems, making the plant ideal for hanging baskets. Fast growing and easy.

Light: Provide 2 to 3 hours of curtain-filtered sunlight in a south, east, or west window.

Water: Keep evenly moist. Water thoroughly and discard drainage.

Humidity: Average indoor humidity levels.

Temperatures: 60° to 65° F at night, 70° to 75° F during the day.

Fertilization: Fertilize lightly throughout the growing season.

Propagation: Take cuttings at any time.

Grooming: Pick off yellowed leaves. Cut back old stems to soil level to promote rejuvenation.

Repotting: Repot as necessary.

Problems: Leaves may die back or dry up in dry air. Growth may be stringy and color poor when light is too low.

Ornithogalum caudatum
Ornithogalum, pregnant-onion, false sea-onion

Although there are many ornithogalums that grow outdoors, only one is popular as a year-round houseplant. It derives its common name of pregnant-onion from the fact that its onionlike bulb, which is above ground, produces offsets just under its skin, causing it to bulge outward. Although grown mainly as a curiosity, it readily produces a tall, though weak-stemmed, flower stalk

with numerous white, star-shaped flowers. The leaves are bright green and straplike, arching gracefully away from the bulb. The leaves, when crushed, are reputed to have a healing effect and have been used as a poultice for cuts.
Light: Keep in direct sunlight for at least 4 hours in winter. Provide curtain-filtered sunlight from a south, east, or west window in summer.
Water: Grows best if allowed to approach dryness before watering. Discard drainage.
Humidity: Average indoor humidity levels.
Temperatures: 60° to 65° F at night, 70° to 85° F during the day.
Fertilization: Fertilize only when plant is growing actively or flowering.
Propagation: Start new plants from the bulblets that develop beside the parent bulb.
Grooming: Remove old leaves as plant goes dormant.
Repotting: Repot after flowering, setting the bulb so that only its base is covered with potting mixture.
Problems: Grows weak and straggly if light is too low.

Osmanthus heterophyllus 'Variegatus'
False-holly, holly osmanthus

The shiny, spine-edged leaves of false-holly do indeed resemble those of the true holly. The variety most often grown has creamy white markings on the leaf edges, which may also be tinged with pink in bright light. The same plant may have both spiny leaves and leaves that are almost round. False-holly rarely blooms indoors.
Light: Provide about 4 hours of curtain-filtered sunlight from a bright south, east, or west window.
Water: Water thoroughly, but allow to dry between waterings.
Humidity: Requires moist air. Use a humidifier for best results.
Temperatures: 50° to 55° F both day and night. Place in a cool, even drafty spot in summer.
Fertilization: Fertilize lightly throughout the growing season.
Propagation: Take stem cuttings in spring; use a rooting hormone.
Grooming: Pinch regularly to obtain bushy growth.

Repotting: Repot infrequently.
Problems: Leaves may die back or dry up in dry air.

Palms

Palms are consistently popular as houseplants. Their graceful fans and rich green color can give even the coldest northern home a tropical air. The family is large and varied, but only a few are available as houseplants. Although they are among the most expensive plants, palms are well worth the investment. They are very tolerant and adapt well to the limited light and controlled temperatures of indoors. You can save money by purchasing small, young plants that will grow slowly into large trees. Some types will flourish for decades.

Most palms are easy to care for and have uniform growing requirements. During the spring and summer growing season, water plants heavily and feed them once a month. Reduce water and stop feeding them in winter. Protect palms from dry air and direct sunlight, especially if you move them outdoors. Do not prune palm trees unless a stem or frond dies. Unlike most plants, palms will produce new growth only from the tip of the stalk. Pinching back this tip or cutting off the newest frond below its point of attachment to the trunk will eliminate all new growth.

Caryota mitis
Fishtail palm

Fishtail palms become large. They have a thick trunk and many spreading fronds, each laden with fans of dark green leaflets. The ribbed texture of the leaflets and their wedged shape account for the common name. Fishtail palm is often used in commercial interiors because it grows relatively slowly and is easy to care for.

Chamaedorea elegans
Parlor palm, bamboo palm, reed palm

Parlor palm (also known as *Neanthe bella*) has handsome, light green fronds. Given enough light, it will bear clusters of yellow flowers among the lower leaves. It is a small palm, eventually

Osmanthus heterophyllus 'Variegatus'

Ornithogalum caudatum

Palm: *Caryota mitis*

Palm: *Chamaedorea elegans*

Palm: *Chamaerops humilis*

Palm: *Chrysalidocarpus lutescens*

Palm: *Howea forsterana*

Palm: *Phoenix roebelenii*

growing to a height of 6 feet, which makes it suitable for entryways and living rooms. *C. erumpens* (bamboo palm) bears clusters of drooping fronds. *C. seifrizii* (reed palm) has clusters of narrow, feathery fronds.

Chamaerops humilis
European fan palm

The European fan palm has fan-shaped leaves about 1 foot wide. The multiple trunks, reaching 4 feet high and taller, are rough and black and grow at an angle from the container.

Chrysalidocarpus lutescens
Areca palm, butterfly palm

The areca palm is a cluster of thin, yellow canes with arching fronds and strap-shaped, shiny green leaflets. It is a medium-sized palm and slow growing.

Howea forsterana
Kentia palm

Outdoors, the popular kentia palm grows to be a very large tree, but indoors it will rarely exceed 7 or 8 feet. Feather-shaped leaves arch outward from sturdy branches to create a full appearance. The leaves scorch easily, so take care to place this plant in the shade if you move it outdoors.

Livistona chinensis
Chinese fan palm

Chinese fan palms are large plants with deeply lobed, fan leaves up to 2 feet across. The plants will eventually grow to 10 feet if given enough room and a large enough container. They will tolerate bright, indirect light. Keep the soil very moist, but not soggy, and keep the plants warm at night.

Phoenix roebelenii
Pygmy date palm

Pygmy date palm is a dwarf, growing to a height of only 4 feet. A delicate-looking plant, its arching, narrow-leaved fronds branch to form a symmetrical shape. Like the other palms, it requires a minimum of attention.

Rhapis
Lady palm

Lady palm features 6- to 12-inch-wide fans of thick, shiny leaflets, 4 to 10 per fan. The fans grow at the ends of thin leafstalks that arch from a brown, hairy trunk. Popular varieties include *R. humilis* and *R. subtilis;* many variegated cultivars are also available.

Care of Palms

Light: Provide at least moderate light but no direct sunlight.
Water: Let plant approach dryness before watering, then water thoroughly and discard drainage.
Humidity: Average indoor humidity levels.
Temperatures: 50° to 55° F at night, 60° to 65° F during the day.
Fertilization: Fertilize all year, more heavily in summer.
Propagation: Start from seeds. Sow in a small pot and transplant seedlings as needed. Usually propagated only by professionals. Some palms can be divided.
Grooming: Pick off yellowed leaves. Wash leaves from time to time.
Repotting: Repot infrequently.
Problems: Poor drainage, too-frequent watering, or standing in water will cause root rot. Spider mites can be a problem, especially if air is too dry.

Pandanus
Screwpine

Screwpine owes its name to its leaves, which spiral upward, corkscrew fashion, in a compact rosette. The leaves resemble corn leaves, but they have prickly edges. Screwpine is a tough, yet graceful plant. Common varieties include *P. veitchii,* its cultivar 'Verde', and *P. utilis.* Some varieties have white, vertical stripes; others have burgundy edges. Aerial roots grow downward, searching for moist soil. This is an almost foolproof, pest-free specimen to add to an indoor plant collection. But be careful with this plant; its prickly leaves can injure both you and plants that are close to it.
Light: In winter, keep in about 4 hours of direct sunlight. In summer, provide curtain-filtered sunlight from a south or west window.

Water: Keep very moist during growth and flowering; at other times, allow to dry between waterings.
Humidity: Requires moist air. Use a humidifier for best results.
Temperatures: 55° to 60° F at night, 70° to 75° F during the day.
Fertilization: Fertilize lightly throughout the growing season.
Propagation: Remove plantlets or rooted side shoots as they form.
Grooming: Wash foliage from time to time. Train aerial roots into soil.
Repotting: Repot in winter or early spring, as needed.
Problems: Dry soil or a high level of soluble salts may damage roots, causing plant to die back.

Pellionia
Pellionia

Pellionias are trailing plants, suitable for small hanging baskets. They are also occasionally used as ground covers in terrariums or bed plantings, because the stems root wherever they contact the soil. The small leaves of most pellionias are borne closely along the stems. The two main species are *P. daveauana* and *P. pulchra.* Many variegated cultivars are available. Keep pellionias warm and out of drafts.
Light: Place in a bright, indirectly lit south, east, or west window.
Water: Keep evenly moist. Water thoroughly and discard drainage.
Humidity: Requires moist air. Use a humidifier for best results.
Temperatures: 55° to 60° F at night, 70° to 75° F during the day.
Fertilization: Fertilize lightly throughout the growing season.
Propagation: Take stem cuttings at any time.
Grooming: Keep to desired height and shape with light pruning or clipping at any time.
Repotting: Repot in winter or early spring, as needed.
Problems: Leaves will scorch if plant is in a draft or dry air. They will drop if soil is too wet or too dry.

Peperomia
Peperomia, baby rubber plant, creeping-buttons, false-philodendron, silverleaf peperomia, watermelon begonia

Peperomia is an extremely varied genus. It offers an astonishing variety of leaf forms, colors, and growth habits. Most

Palm: *Rhapis*

Pandanus veitchii

Pellionia pulchra

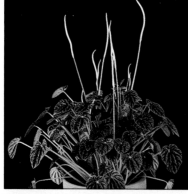

Peperomia caperata 'Emerald Ripple'

Peperomia obtusifolia (Upright)

Peperomia (Trailing)

Persea americana

peperomias are easy-to-grow, small plants ideally suited to windowsills and plant shelves. Under good conditions, they produce curious, if not necessarily striking, creamy white blooms the shape of mouse tails.

Clumping Peperomias

Clumping peperomias are a mass of leaves on short stems originating from the clump. *P. argyreia,* formerly known as *P. sandersii* (watermelon begonia), has thick, smooth, almost round leaves striped with green and silver. *P. caperata* 'Emerald Ripple' has small, dark, heart-shaped leaves with a deeply corrugated surface. This plant has many different cultivars, including dwarf types and variegates. *P. griseoargentea* (silverleaf peperomia) has a similarly corrugated surface but is silvery gray throughout. Another interesting one is *P. orba* 'Princess Astrid', a dwarf plant with spoon-shaped, apple green leaves covered with fine hairs. Generally speaking, clumping peperomias are more susceptible to crown rot than other peperomias.

Trailing Peperomias

Trailing peperomias have weak, pendant stems. The best known is *P. scandens* 'Variegata' (false-philodendron), which bears 2-inch, heart-shaped leaves with a broad cream edge on arching stems. It's indeed much like a variegated version of the heart-leaf philodendron. *P. rotundifolia* var. *pilosior* (creeping-buttons) is very different; it produces thin, weak, zigzagging stems and tiny, round, domed leaves with green and silver markings.

Upright Peperomias

Upright peperomias have visible stems and generally grow upward, although they become prostrate as the stems become heavier. Since they branch readily at the base, they are usually pruned back when they start to droop. The best known is *P. obtusifolia* (baby rubber plant), which bears thick stems and waxy, obtuse leaves of varying sizes. It has many cultivars with different forms of variegation, from light speckling to large zones of yellow or cream.

P. magnoliifolia is similar to *P. obtusifolia* but has larger leaves. Quite different is *P. verticillata*, with its shiny, sharply pointed leaves in whorls of 3 to 5 along an upright, reddish stem.

Care of Peperomias

Light: Place in a bright, indirectly lit south, east, or west window.
Water: Let plant dry slightly before watering, then water thoroughly and discard drainage.
Humidity: Requires moist air. Use a humidifier for best results.
Temperatures: 55° to 60° F at night, 70° to 75° F during the day.
Fertilization: Fertilize lightly throughout the growing season.
Propagation: Divide, or grow from stem cuttings. Many peperomias with thick leaves will also grow from leaf cuttings.
Grooming: Pick off yellowed leaves. Prune or pinch upright and trailing kinds as needed.
Repotting: Repot as needed.
Problems: Subject to crown rot in overly moist conditions. Will get spindly and weak if light is too low.

Persea americana
Avocado

Avocados are popular classroom plants because the seeds germinate so easily when partially submerged in water. They make attractive pot plants after several years of pinching back to encourage branching. Give them plenty of light so they do not get spindly. The plant may require staking. It will not flower or set fruit indoors.
Light: Provide 4 hours or more of direct sunlight from a south window.
Water: Keep evenly moist. Water thoroughly and discard drainage.
Humidity: Requires moist air. Use a humidifier for best results.
Temperatures: 55° to 60° F at night, 70° to 75° F during the day.
Fertilization: Fertilize all year, more heavily in summer.
Propagation: Put fruit pit halfway into water, at any time. When well rooted, place in a pot with soil, keeping half the pit above the soil.
Grooming: Pinch back stem tips routinely to encourage branching. Stake to keep plant upright.

Repotting: Repot at any time. Keep half of pit above soil.
Problems: Leaves will scorch if plant is in a draft or dry air.

Philodendrons

No other group of plants is as widely used indoors as philodendrons. The great variety of sizes and growth habits (vines, shrubs, and trees), as well as the uniquely shaped glossy leaves, give the indoor gardener many choices for almost any situation. And you don't have to worry about providing perfect growing conditions. Originally from South American tropical forests, philodendrons are strong, tolerant plants that don't need a lot of sunlight.

The 200 or so species are classified according to their growth habit, as either climbers or nonclimbers. The climbing species are the ones most commonly grown in the home. The name is a bit of a misnomer, though, since none of them climb well indoors. They must be tied to supports as they grow, and the aerial roots tied to the stem or directed to the ground for further support.

The nonclimbing philodendrons can become large plants 6 to 8 feet tall. Their leaves, of varying shapes, extend from self-supporting trunks. These plants are ideal for offices or for large rooms with high ceilings.

A few basic techniques will keep your philodendron healthy and thriving. It will do best in bright light, but it doesn't need direct sunlight. Water regularly to keep the soil moist, and wash the leaves about once a month. An undersized pot, low temperatures, or poor drainage will cause leaves to yellow and drop. However, it is natural for the climbing types to drop their lower leaves as they grow.

Philodendron bipinnatifidum
Twice-cut philodendron, fiddleleaf philodendron

The deeply cut, star-shaped leaves of twice-cut philodendron are large. It is a nonclimbing type, so it needs no support.

Philodendron hastatum
Spade-leaf philodendron

Spade-leaf philodendron is a lush, evergreen, climbing vine with aerial roots.

Deeply veined, bright green leaves take the shape of giant spearheads, 8 to 12 inches long.

Philodendron pertusum
See *Monstera deliciosa*

Philodendron 'Red Emerald'
Red Emerald philodendron

Red Emerald philodendron has red stems topped with bright green, yellow-veined, spear-shaped leaves. It's a climbing kind.

Philodendron scandens oxycardium
Heart-leaf philodendron

Heart-leaf philodendron, also known as *P. cordatum,* has many glossy, deep green leaves. It is the most popular philodendron grown in the United States. Since it's a vigorous climber, train it on a column, frame a window with it, or hang it from a beamed ceiling. This plant does fine in the shade.

Philodendron selloum
Lacy-tree philodendron

A nonclimbing, cut-leaf species, lacy-tree philodendron is often used to decorate offices. As it ages, the cuts deepen and cause the leaves to ruffle.

Care of Philodendrons

Light: Provide at least moderate light but no direct sunlight.
Water: Keep evenly moist. Water thoroughly and discard drainage.
Humidity: Average indoor humidity levels.
Temperatures: 50° to 55° F at night, 60° to 65° F during the day.
Fertilization: Fertilize all year, more heavily in summer.
Propagation: Take stem cuttings at any time, or air-layer climbing types.
Grooming: Keep climbing types to desired height and shape with light pruning or clipping at any time. Direct aerial roots to soil or remove them if they are unattractive. Clean the leaves from time to time.
Repotting: Repot in winter or early spring, as needed.
Problems: It is natural for climbing philodendrons to drop lower leaves.

Philodendron scandens oxycardium

Philodendron selloum

Philodendron hastatum

Philodendron 'Red Emerald'

Pilea cadierei

Pilea 'Moon Valley'

Pittosporum tobira

Pilea

Aluminum-plant, artillery plant, creeping-charlie, panamiga, friendship-plant

There are more than 200 widely varied species in the *Pilea* genus. Most of the ones that are suitable for indoor gardening are moderately sized herbaceous plants. They grow about a foot tall and have variegated leaves with depressed veins, giving them a quilted appearance. The dark green leaves of many species are tinged with red, silver, or copper. Others bear a resemblance to their wild cousins, the stinging nettles, but are harmless. Still others have a creeping or trailing habit that makes them particularly useful in hanging baskets. Some species produce inconspicuous flowers in summer.

P. cadierei (aluminum-plant) is one of the most popular species. Its wafered, green leaves look like they have been brushed with silver paint. *P. cadierei* 'Silver Tree' is similar, with bronze leaves. *P. involucrata* (panamiga or friendship-plant) is more compact, with thick clusters of broad leaves. They are yellow-green with a coppery sheen above, and they have a rich, velvety texture. *P. involucrata* 'Norfolk' is similar to *P. involucrata* but with larger leaves in deep bronze and bright silver markings. *P. nummulariifolia* (hairy creeping-charlie) is very different from the others, with its small, pale green, rounded leaves and creeping stems. It makes a good choice for hanging baskets. *P. depressa* (shiny creeping-charlie) resembles *P. nummulariifolia,* but has smaller leaves and a smooth, hairless surface. *P. microphylla* (artillery-plant) bears arching, upright, green stems and tiny, fleshy, apple green leaves. It gets its common name from the fact that its tiny flowers shoot out pollen within seconds after being watered. Pileas are most attractive when young and should be pruned back severely or started anew from cuttings on a regular basis.

Light: Place in a bright, indirectly lit south, east, or west window.

Water: Keep evenly moist. Water thoroughly and discard drainage.

Humidity: Requires moist air. Use a humidifier for best results. Small varieties do well in terrariums.

Temperatures: 65° to 70° F at night, 75° to 80° F during the day.

Fertilization: Fertilize lightly throughout the growing season.

Propagation: Take stem cuttings at any time.

Grooming: Start new plants to replace old specimens as they get weak. Keep to desired size and shape with pruning or clipping at any time.

Repotting: Repot each year in late spring.

Problems: Subject to crown rot in overly moist conditions. Very susceptible to cold drafts or cold irrigation water. Will get spindly and weak in low light.

Pittosporum tobira

Japanese pittosporum

Japanese pittosporums are widely used in commercial interiors because they are tolerant of moderate light and many diverse indoor environments. They are woody shrubs that eventually get quite large. Their glossy leaves somewhat resemble those of a rhododendron. In ample light, the plant may bloom in the spring; its flowers have a fragrance similar to that of orange blossoms. A variegated form is available, *P. tobira* 'Variegata'.

Light: Place in a bright, indirectly lit south, east, or west window.

Water: Let plant approach dryness before watering, then water thoroughly and discard drainage.

Humidity: Average indoor humidity levels.

Temperatures: 40° to 45° F at night, 60° to 65° F during the day.

Fertilization: Fertilize lightly throughout the growing season.

Propagation: Take cuttings from stems or shoots that have recently matured, or air-layer.

Grooming: Keep to desired height and shape with light pruning or clipping at any time.

Repotting: Repot infrequently, in winter or early spring when needed.

Problems: Will not bloom if light is too low. Subject to scale and mealybugs.

Plectranthus

Swedish ivy

Although commonly known as Swedish ivy, plectranthus is neither from Sweden nor an ivy. The name comes from its popularity in Scandinavia as a hanging and trailing plant. Spikes of white flowers appear occasionally. *P. australis* has waxy, leathery, bright green leaves and a trailing habit. *P. coleoides* 'Marginatus' is not as trailing as other species. Its leaves are green and grayish with cream edges. *P. oertendahlii* has leaves of silver and purple with scalloped edges.

These striking plants are fairly tolerant and require a minimum of care. Place them in bright light, and water regularly.

Light: Place in a bright, indirectly lit south, east, or west window.

Water: Keep evenly moist. Water thoroughly and discard drainage.

Humidity: Average indoor humidity levels.

Temperatures: 55° to 60° F at night, 70° to 75° F during the day.

Fertilization: Fertilize all year, more heavily in summer.

Propagation: Take cuttings from stems or shoots that have recently matured.

Grooming: Pinch back stem tips of young or regrowing plants to improve form, being careful not to remove flower buds. Start new plants to replace old specimens when they get weak.

Repotting: Repot at any time.

Problems: Poor drainage, too-frequent watering, or standing in water will cause root rot. Dry soil or a high level of soluble salts may damage roots, causing plant to die back.

Podocarpus macrophyllus var. 'Maki'
Podocarpus, Japanese yew

A more pleasing compact shrub than *P. macrophyllus* var. 'Maki' is hard to find. A group of branches supports spirals of thin green leaves, each 3 inches long. As the branches lengthen, they gradually arch downward. Some species grow to 10 feet.

In the right environment podocarpus will thrive for many years. It's a slow-growing, tolerant plant that does best in cool temperatures and bright, filtered light. Control its size by pinching back the tips; this will encourage branching and bushiness.

Light: Place in a bright, indirectly lit south, east, or west window.

Water: Let plant approach dryness before watering, then water thoroughly and discard drainage.

Humidity: Average indoor humidity levels.

Temperatures: 50° to 55° F at night, 60° to 65° F during the day.

Fertilization: Fertilize lightly throughout the growing season.

Propagation: Take cuttings from stems or shoots that have recently matured.

Grooming: Keep to desired height and shape with light pruning or clipping at any time.

Repotting: Repot in winter or early spring, as needed.

Problems: Leaves will scorch if plant is in a draft or dry air. Poor drainage, too-frequent watering, or standing in water will cause root rot.

Polyscias
Aralia, balfour aralia, ming aralia

Aralias are woody shrubs frequently grown indoors for their lacy, often variegated foliage. They grow large and bushy and are popular in commercial interiors. The leaves of some cultivars are aromatic when crushed or bruised. *P. fruticosa* (ming aralia) has finely divided leaves and can reach a height of 8 feet. Its cultivar 'Elegans' is smaller, with extremely dense foliage. *P. balfouriana* 'Marginata' has leaves edged with white. The leaves of *P. balfouriana* 'Pennockii' are white to light green with green spots. *P. guilfoylei* 'Victoriae' is compact, with deeply divided leaves edged in white. Give aralias plenty of room, and prune them frequently to achieve good form.

Light: Provide at least moderate light but no direct sunlight.

Water: Let plant approach dryness before watering, then water thoroughly and discard drainage.

Humidity: Requires moist air. Use a humidifier for best results.

Temperatures: 55° to 60° F at night, 70° to 75° F during the day.

Fertilization: Fertilize lightly throughout the growing season.

Propagation: Take stem cuttings.

Grooming: Keep to desired height and shape with light pruning or clipping at any time.

Repotting: Repot in winter or early spring, as needed.

Plectranthus australis

Podocarpus macrophyllus

Polyscias fruticosa 'Elegans'

Radermachera sinica

Saxifraga stolonifera

Scirpus cernuus

Problems: Will get spindly and weak if light is too low. Poor drainage, too-frequent watering, or standing in water will cause root rot. Susceptible to mites, scale, and mealybugs.

Radermachera sinica
China-doll

The shiny, bright green leaves of *R. sinica* are doubly compound, giving it a delicate, fern appearance, although its stems are woody. In the nursery, it is usually planted 3 to a pot for a fuller look, and treated with a growth retardant, which decreases the distance between the leaves, making the plant more compact. The effect of the retardant may last for over a year; as it wears off the plant will return to its more open natural growth habit.

Light: Provide 2 to 3 hours of curtain-filtered sunlight through a south, east, or west window.

Water: Keep evenly moist. Water thoroughly and discard drainage.

Humidity: Average indoor humidity levels.

Temperatures: 60° to 65° F at night, 70° to 75° F during the day.

Fertilization: Fertilize lightly throughout the growing season.

Propagation: Commercially, it is grown from seeds, but it can be started from cuttings.

Grooming: Pick off yellowed leaves. To keep it compact, pinch regularly when the effect of the growth hormone has worn off.

Repotting: Repot as necessary.

Problems: Leaves may dry up if soil dries out between waterings.

Saxifraga stolonifera
Strawberry-geranium,
strawberry-begonia

Saxifraga stolonifera is neither a geranium nor a begonia; its names come from the shape, resembling geranium leaves, and colors of the foliage, resembling that of begonias. One variegated cultivar, *S. stolonifera* 'Tricolor', is available, but is not as easy to maintain as the species. Strawberry-geraniums are best suited for ground covers or hanging baskets. They divide quickly, sending out runners that form plantlets much as strawberries do. In summer, small, white flowers appear on long stalks above the foliage. Many gardeners display these plants on a patio during the summer. If you take them outdoors, make sure they are pest free before you bring them back indoors.

Light: Place in a bright, indirectly lit south, east, or west window.

Water: Let plant approach dryness before watering, then water thoroughly and discard drainage.

Humidity: Average indoor humidity levels.

Temperatures: 50° to 55° F at night, 60° to 65° F during the day.

Fertilization: Fertilize lightly throughout the growing season.

Propagation: Start new plants by dividing an old specimen, or remove any plantlets or rooted side shoots as they form.

Grooming: Cut flower stalks if you wish.

Repotting: Repot each year. Cut back and repot when flowering stops.

Problems: Will get spindly and weak if light is too low. Dry soil or a high level of soluble salts may damage roots, causing plant to die back. Leaves will scorch if plant is in a draft or dry air.

Scindapsus aureus

See *Epipremnum aureum*

Scirpus cernuus
Miniature bulrush

Miniature bulrush is a graceful, grassy plant, whose thin, green stems arch over and hang downward as they grow, making it a good choice for a hanging basket. Each stem bears a tiny, cream flower at its tip, which, although it adds a little interest to the plant's appearance, is not showy enough for the plant to be considered as anything other than a foliage plant.

Light: Place in a bright, indirectly lit south, east, or west window.

Water: Keep thoroughly moist at all times; can stand in water permanently.

Humidity: Average indoor humidity levels.

Temperatures: 60° to 65° F at night, 70° to 75° F during the day.

Fertilization: Fertilize lightly throughout the growing season.

Propagation: Divide in spring.

Grooming: Pick off yellowed leaves.
Repotting: Repot in spring as necessary.
Problems: Leaves may die back or dry up in dry air. Plant will die if soil dries out.

Selaginella
Spike-moss, moss-fern, sweat-plant, spreading club-moss

Selaginella is a group of primitive, mossy plants that are actually more closely related to ferns than to true mosses. They are popular terrarium plants; they don't do well in the open air. Some species, such as *S. martensii,* grow upright for about half their height, then spread, making small forests of miniature trees. Others, such as *S. pallescens* (up to 1 foot) and *S. kraussiana* 'Brownii' (a true miniature at only 1 inch high) form soft mats. There are various variegated and golden-leaved cultivars.
Light: Place in a bright, indirectly lit south, east, or west window.
Water: Keep evenly moist. Water thoroughly and discard drainage.
Humidity: Needs extremely high humidity levels. Does poorly outside a terrarium.
Temperatures: 65° to 70° F at night, 75° to 80° F during the day.
Fertilization: Fertilize lightly throughout the growing season.
Propagation: Take stem cuttings in spring.
Grooming: Trim any overgrown sections.
Repotting: Repot in spring as necessary.
Problems: Leaves may die back or dry up in dry air.

Senecio
Waxvine, German ivy, parlor-ivy

Although the genus *Senecio* is a vast one, including both flowering annuals and succulents, the two houseplants mentioned here are similar hanging plants grown for their foliage. *S. macroglossus* is generally available only in one of its variegated forms: *S. macroglossus* 'Medio-picta', with a splotch of bright yellow in the center of each leaf, or *S. macroglossus* 'Variegatum', with a creamy yellow border to

its leaves. The leaves are shiny with 3 to 5 pointed lobes and are borne on purple stems. In shape and size, they resemble those of true ivy. *S. mikanioides* is similar to *s. macroglossus* but has entirely green leaves with 5 to 7 lobes.
Light: Provide about 4 hours of curtain-filtered sunlight from a bright south, east, or west window.
Water: Water thoroughly, then allow to dry between waterings. Water sparingly during the rest period.
Humidity: Average indoor humidity levels.
Temperatures: During the growing season, 65° to 70° F at night, 75° to 80° F during the day. During the winter rest period, 50° to 55° F at night, 60° to 65° F during the day.
Fertilization: Fertilize lightly throughout the growing season.
Propagation: Take stem cuttings at any time.
Grooming: Pick off yellowed leaves and prune overly long stems.
Repotting: Repot in spring as necessary.
Problems: Subject to spider mites in dry air.

Soleirolia soleirolii
Baby's tears

Baby's tears, often sold as *Helxine soleirolii,* is a compact creeper that has tiny, delicate, rounded leaves on thin, trailing stems. It grows into a dense mat and makes a good terrarium ground cover. It thrives in high humidity.
Light: Place in a bright, indirectly lit south, east, or west window.
Water: Keep evenly moist. Water thoroughly and discard drainage.
Humidity: Requires moist air. Use a humidifier for best results.
Temperatures: 50° to 55° F at night, 60° to 65° F during the day.
Fertilization: Fertilize all year, more heavily in summer.
Propagation: Start new plants by dividing an old specimen, or grow easily from cuttings, pressing them into moist rooting mix.

Selaginella kraussiana

Senecio macroglossus 'Variegatum'

Senecio mikanioides

Soleirolia soleirolii

Rhoeo spathacea

Grooming: Keep to desired height and shape with light pruning or clipping at any time.
Repotting: Repot at any time.
Problems: Dry soil or a high level of soluble salts may damage roots, causing plant to die back.

Sonerila margeritacea
Sonerila

Sonerilas are small plants. They have fleshy stems and foliage that is silver on top and reddish on the underside. The plants are very sensitive to dry air and are best suited to a terrarium or other humid location. Given ample light, sonerilas occasionally produce clusters of small, lavender flowers.
Light: Place in a bright, indirectly lit south, east, or west window.
Water: Keep evenly moist. Water thoroughly and discard drainage.
Humidity: Requires moist air. Use a humidifier for best results.
Temperatures: 55° to 60° F at night, 70° to 75° F during the day.
Fertilization: Fertilize lightly throughout the growing season.
Propagation: Take stem cuttings at any time.
Grooming: Pinch back stem tips of young or regrowing plants to improve form, being careful not to remove flower buds.
Repotting: Repot in winter or early spring, as needed.
Problems: Leaves will scorch if plant is in a draft or dry air. Poor drainage, too-frequent watering, or standing in water will cause root rot.

Spiderworts

Wandering-Jew, inch-plant, spiderwort—these are all common names for the popular and easily grown houseplants in the *Commelinaceae,* or Spiderwort, family. They belong to the genera *Callisia, Gibasis, Setcreasea, Tradescantia,* and *Zebrina* and have such similar needs and growth habits they are often grouped together.

Spiderworts have boat-shaped leaves of varying lengths borne alternately along trailing stems. All of them flower seasonally, with small, three-sepaled blooms, but most are grown strictly for their colorful or variegated foliage. They are used as ground covers, in hanging baskets, or as trailing plants on shelves. Pinch back the stem tips and remove old, unattractive stems frequently to prevent legginess or a spindly appearance. Stems of the variegated spiderworts often revert to the nonvariegated form. These should be pinched out.

Callisia
Striped inch-plant

Callisia elegans is very similar to *Tradescantia* and shares the same common name. The leaves are olive green with white stripes.

Gibasis geniculata
Tahitian bridal-veil

The tiny-leaved Tahitian bridal-veil is the only spiderwort that blooms with any frequency. It bears delicate, white flowers on thin stalks in spring and summer. For more information, see the listing for *Gibasis* in the "Flowering Houseplants" section.

Rhoeo spathacea
Moses-in-the-cradle, boat-lily, oyster plant

The common names for *Rhoeo spathacea* (now known as *Tradescantia spathacea*) come from the odd way it bears flowers. At the base of the terminal leaves on the shoots, small, white blooms appear within cupped bracts. The foliage is striking: It is green on top and deep purple or maroon beneath. The cultivar *R. spathacea* 'Variegata' is especially noteworthy. The plant has cane stems that trail as they get older, so it is generally grown in a hanging basket. Fertilize lightly, and flush the soil occasionally to keep the older leaves from dropping. Unlike most spiderworts, Moses-in-the-cradle is not propagated by cuttings, but by division.

Setcreasea pallida
Purple-heart

Purple-heart (*Setcreasea pallida*, more correctly *Tradescantia pallida*) is slower growing than most spiderworts, requires less pinching, but it needs more light to bring out the attractive deep purple that gives it its name. The bright pink flowers are short-lived but nonetheless very attractive.

Tradescantia
Striped inch-plant, wandering-Jew

The most common *Tradescantia* varieties are variegated with white or cream bands. Among them are *T. albiflora* Albovittata, *T. blossfeldiana* 'Variegata', and *T. fluminensis* 'Variegata'. *T. sillamontana* differs from the other tradescantias in that it bears entirely green leaves, which are covered in woolly, white hair.

Zebrina pendula
Wandering-Jew

Zebrina pendula, now *Tradescantia zebrina*, has shiny green leaves with broad, iridescent silver bands and purple undersides. Among the various variegated forms, *Z. pendula* 'Quadricolor' is the most colorful; it's heavily striped with white and pink.

Care of Spiderworts

Light: Provide at least moderate light but no direct sunlight. *Setcreasea pallida* prefers some direct sunlight.
Water: Let plant approach dryness before watering, then water thoroughly and discard drainage.
Humidity: Average indoor humidity levels.
Temperatures: 50° to 55° F at night, 65° to 70° F during the day.
Fertilization: Fertilize all year, more heavily in summer.
Propagation: Take stem cuttings at any time.
Grooming: Cut back overly long stems to stimulate regrowth from base. Pinch stem tips frequently. Remove dried leaves.
Repotting: Repot at any time.

Zebrina pendula

Setcreasea pallida

Syngonium podophyllum

Synadenium grantii 'Rubra'

Strobilanthes dyeranus

Problems: Will get spindly and weak if light is too low. Dry soil or a high level of soluble salts may damage roots, causing plant to die back.

Strobilanthes dyeranus
Persian-shield

The narrow, lance-shaped, quilted leaves of Persian-shield are heavily marbled with rich purple and highlighted with iridescent blue markings. The underside of the leaf is deep wine red. Pale blue flowers are easily produced, but should be eliminated, as they weaken this fast-growing shrub.
Light: Place in a bright, indirectly lit south, east, or west window.
Water: Water thoroughly, then allow to dry between waterings. Water sparingly during the rest period.
Humidity: Requires moist air. Use a humidifier for best results.
Temperatures: 65° to 70° F at night, 75° to 80° F during the day.
Fertilization: Fertilize lightly throughout the growing season.
Propagation: Take stem cuttings in spring.
Grooming: Prune regularly to rejuvenate plant; it ages poorly.
Repotting: Repot in spring as necessary.
Problems: Leaves may die back or dry up in dry air.

Synadenium grantii 'Rubra'
African milkbush

A borderline succulent, the African milkbush makes an attractive, fast-growing indoor tree or shrub. The stem is thick, and the leaves are spoon-shaped, measuring 4 to 6 inches in length. They are irregularly splashed with dull red, sometimes to the point where the whole leaf is burgundy. This is an extremely adaptable plant; it will tolerate just about all indoor conditions.
Light: Place in a bright, indirectly lit south, east, or west window.
Water: Water thoroughly, then allow to dry between waterings.
Humidity: Average indoor humidity levels.

Temperatures: 65° to 70° F at night , 75° to 80° F during the day.
Fertilization: Fertilize lightly throughout the growing season.
Propagation: Take stem cuttings at any time.
Grooming: Pick off yellowed leaves. Prune as necessary to keep plant within bounds.
Repotting: Repot in spring as necessary.
Problems: Lower leaves may drop if plant dries out.

Syngonium podophyllum
Syngonium, arrowhead vine

Arrowhead vine closely resembles its relatives the climbing philodendrons in both appearance and care requirements. An unusual feature is the change that occurs in the leaf shape as the plant ages. Young leaves are 3 inches long, arrow-shaped, and borne at the ends of erect stalks. They are dark green and may have bold, silvery white variegation. With age, the leaves become lobed, and the stems begin to climb. Eventually the variegation disappears, and each leaf fans into several leaflets. Older leaves may have as many as 11 leaflets. All stages of leaf development occur together on mature plants.

Arrowhead vines do best in a warm, moist environment protected from direct sunlight. Older climbing stems require support; a moss stick works well. To retain the juvenile leaf form and variegation, prune the climbing stems and aerial roots as they appear. Popular cultivars include 'Emerald Gem', 'White Butterfly', and 'Pink Allusion'.
Light: Place in a bright, indirectly lit south, east, or west window.
Water: Keep very moist during growth; at other times, allow to dry between waterings.
Humidity: Requires moist air. Use a humidifier for best results.
Temperatures: 55° to 60° F at night, 70° to 75° F during the day.
Fertilization: Fertilize lightly throughout the growing season.
Propagation: Take cuttings from stems or shoots that have recently matured.

Grooming: Keep to desired height and shape with light pruning or clipping at any time.
Repotting: Repot in winter or early spring, as needed.
Problems: Poor drainage, too-frequent watering, or standing in water will cause root rot. Older climbing stems require support.

Tetrastigma voinieranum
Chestnut vine, lizard-plant

Chestnut-vine is a massive indoor vine suited to large spaces. Its leaves are composed of 4 to 6 (usually 5) coarsely toothed leaflets, each measuring 4 to 8 inches in length. The stems are thick and bear clinging tendrils that allow the plant to climb nearby objects.
Light: Place in a bright, indirectly lit south, east, or west window.
Water: Water thoroughly, then allow to dry between waterings.
Humidity: Average indoor humidity levels.
Temperatures: 65° to 70° F at night, 75° to 80° F during the day.
Fertilization: Fertilize lightly throughout the growing season.
Propagation: Take stem cuttings in spring.
Grooming: Pick off yellowed leaves.
Repotting: Repot in spring as necessary.
Problems: Entire sections often drop off for no apparent reason, but are quickly replaced.

Tolmiea menziesii
Piggyback plant

Piggyback plants are popular with indoor gardeners because of their plantlets, which sprout over the top of the foliage at the junctures of the leaf blades and petioles. Under proper conditions, the trailing stems will quickly produce a large plant suitable for a hanging basket or a pedestal. A variegated form (T. menziesii 'Variegata') is available. These plants must be kept cool at night, and constantly moist. They need only light fertilization and will not tolerate drafts or dry air.

Light: Place in a bright, indirectly lit south, east, or west window.
Water: Keep evenly moist. Water thoroughly and discard drainage.
Humidity: Requires moist air. Use a humidifier for best results.
Temperatures: 40° to 45° F at night, 60° to 65° F during the day.
Fertilization: Fertilize lightly throughout the growing season.
Propagation: Remove plantlets as they form.
Grooming: Keep to the desired height and shape with light pruning or clipping at any time.
Repotting: Repot each year.
Problems: Leaves will scorch if plant is in a draft or dry air. Dry soil or a high level of soluble salts may damage roots, causing plant to die back and making it prone to infestations of spider mites.

Xanthosoma lindenii
Indian kale, spoonflower

Strikingly beautiful, arrow-shaped leaves with ivory white veins characterize Indian kale, a relative of the philodendron. It grows from tubers, much like another close relative, the caladium, and like the latter, enters into a dormant state in winter. At that time, it requires only enough water to keep it from drying out entirely. Besides X. lindenii, there are several other species and hybrids that make suitable houseplants.
Light: Place in a bright, indirectly lit south, east, or west window.
Water: Water thoroughly during the growing season, allowing plant to dry slightly between waterings. Keep almost dry during dormancy.
Humidity: Requires moist air. Use a humidifier for best results.
Temperatures: 65° to 70° F at night, 75° to 80° F during the day.
Fertilization: Fertilize lightly throughout the growing season.
Propagation: Divide in spring, at the end of dormancy.
Grooming: Pick off yellowed leaves.
Repotting: Repot infrequently.
Problems: Subject to crown rot in overly moist conditions. Leaves will wilt or become damaged by dry air.

Tolmiea menziesii

Xanthosoma

Cereus peruvianus

Cephalocereus senilis

Echinocactus grusonii

Mammillaria bocasana

Notocactus leninghausii

Cacti and Succulents

Over millions of years, cacti and succulents, stubborn individualists of the plant world, adapted to great climatic changes. Many stored water in their stems or leaves. Others abandoned the land and took to the trees as epiphytes, using their roots for gripping instead of taking nourishment. Some developed disproportionately thick rootstocks. Others adapted to rocky, frigid climates. In the course of developing such special talents, these plants evolved into unique and wonderful shapes, colors, and textures.

The apartment gardener who has only a sunny windowsill, the commuter who needs patient plants, the collector looking for the unusual—all will find succulents absorbing and satisfying plants. This section describes some of the more popular species of succulents, of which cacti are a part, and gives general care information.

Cacti

The cactus family encompasses more than 2,000 plants. The distinguishing characteristic of cacti is not spines, but *areoles*, small sunken or raised spots on cactus stems from which spines, flowers, and leaves grow. Some of the most popular cacti are described below, divided into desert cacti and epiphytic cacti according to their cultural requirements.

Desert Cacti

Desert cacti are extremely tolerant plants, but they do need a very porous soil that drains well. Most desert cacti need a cool, dry, dormant period in winter to bloom well.

Cephalocereus senilis
Oldman cactus

An upright, cylindrical cactus, oldman cactus can reach a height of 10 feet and a diameter of 8 to 10 inches. Its gray-green body develops soft, furry spines while still immature. Rose, funnel-shaped flowers are borne atop the cactus when it is several years old. It grows slowly and is good on a windowsill when young.

Cereus
Peruvian apple, curiosity-plant

Cereus species have deeply ribbed, blue-green stems. Certain cultivars, such as *C. peruvianus* 'Monstrosus', are noted for the numerous deformed growths that cover the plant. They can reach a height of 20 feet. Large flowers, borne all along the stems in summer, open at night.

Echinocactus grusonii
Golden barrel cactus

A popular globe-shaped cactus, golden barrel cactus has yellow spines prominently borne on its stem ribs. It grows slowly but can reach 3 feet in diameter. Yellow, bell-shaped flowers are borne on the top central ring in the summer.

Mammillaria
Pincushion cactus, snowball cactus, little candles cactus, silver cluster cactus, rose pincushion

The numerous and extremely diverse members of the *Mammillaria* genus include globular and cylindrical forms. They range from tiny, individual heads only a few inches wide to massive clumps. Unlike other cacti, mammillaria blooms grow from the joints of tubercles, or nodules, forming a ring around the top of the plant. Flowering occurs from March to October.

Notocactus
Ball cactus

The dark green ball cacti have spines that may be white to yellowish white or reddish brown and bell-shaped flowers that are mostly yellow (though some are red-purple). *N. leninghausii*, one of the largest species, can reach 3 feet tall. This plant is a good choice for beginners.

Opuntia
Opuntia, bunny-ears

A flattened stem resembling a pad characterizes most of the *Opuntia* genus. Small tufts of spines create a dotted pattern over the surface of the plant. *O. microdasys* (bunny-ears) has flat pads growing out of the top of large mature pads. *O. salmiana* will produce snow-white flowers in summer.

Care of Desert Cacti

Light: Provide at least 4 hours of curtain-filtered sunlight from a bright south, east, or west window.
Water: During dormancy, water sparingly. At other times, water thoroughly, but allow to dry between waterings.
Humidity: Dry air is generally not harmful, but keep plant out of drafts.
Temperatures: To set flower buds, 40° to 45° F at night, 60° to 65° F during the day. At other times, 50° to 55° F at night, 65° to 70° F during the day.
Fertilization: Fertilize lightly during the spring and summer growing season with a low-nitrogen fertilizer.
Propagation: Start new plants by dividing an old specimen. Seeds are available, but can be more difficult than division.
Grooming: None usually needed.
Repotting: Repot infrequently, into a very porous soil mix.
Problems: Poor drainage, too-frequent watering, or standing in water will cause root rot. Will not bloom in low light.

Epiphytic Cacti

Epiphytic cacti adapted to their jungle environment by using their aerial roots for clinging to trees. They often make spectacular hanging-basket plants. Most epiphytic cacti need a cool, dry, dormant period in the winter to bloom well.

Epicactus
Orchid cactus

The orchid cactus is grown indoors in hanging baskets. Its branches are flat and arch outward from a central crown. It is grown primarily for its large, showy flowers, which appear anywhere on the stem in spring and early summer.

Rhipsalidopsis gaertneri
Easter cactus

Easter cactus (also known as *Schlumbergera gaertneri*) is often confused with *S. × buckleyi*, but it droops less, and its stems and joints bear scarlet, sharp-tipped, upright or horizontal flowers. It blooms at Eastertime, and sometimes again in early fall.

Schlumbergera
Holiday cactus, Christmas cactus, Thanksgiving cactus

Schlumbergeras are native to the tropical forests of South America. *S. × buckleyi* (Christmas cactus) has arching, drooping, bright green stems which are spineless, but scalloped, and bear tubular flowers in a wide range of colors at Christmastime. *S. truncata* (Thanksgiving cactus) flowers earlier in winter. Schlumbergeras require a rich, porous soil. To promote flowering, place plants outdoors for a time during the fall.

Care of Epiphytic Cacti

Light: Place in a bright but indirectly lit south, east, or west window.
Water: Keep very moist during growth and flowering; at other times, allow to dry between waterings.
Humidity: Average indoor humidity levels.
Temperatures: To set flower buds, 40° to 45° F at night, 60° to 65° F during the day. At other times 50° to 55° F at night, 65° to 70° F during the day.
Fertilization: Fertilize only when plant is growing actively or flowering.
Propagation: Take cuttings from recently matured stems or shoots when plant is not in flower.
Grooming: Prune after flowering.
Repotting: Repot infrequently, into a humus-rich soil.
Problems: Dry soil or a high level of soluble salts may cause dieback.

Opuntia microdasys

Epicactus 'Bella Vista'

Rhipsalidopsis gaertneri

Schlumbergera bridgesii

Agave victoriae-reginae

Aloe barbadensis

Crassula argentea

Echeveria elegans

Euphorbia milii

Kalanchoe blossfeldiana

Succulents

Succulents are generally easy to care for and are a good starting point for beginning gardeners. All succulents require the same basic care: a porous, fast-draining soil; plenty of sunlight, good air circulation, and plenty of water. During the winter they must go dormant in a cool, dry environment to bloom the following season.

Agave
Agave, century plant

Agaves are large plants with thick, pointed leaves. Several of the smaller types, such as *A. victoriae-reginae* (painted century plant), are particularly suitable for indoor gardening. Agaves grow very slowly but need good light. Keep them drier in winter to give them a moderate dormancy period. Repot very infrequently. After a plant matures it may produce a tall flower spike.

Aloe
Aloe, torch-plant, lace aloe, medicine-plant, burn aloe, tiger aloe

There is great diversity among the plants in the *Aloe* genus. *A. aristata* (torch-plant, lace aloe) is a dwarf species that has stemless rosettes edged with soft, white spines or teeth. In winter it bears orange-red flowers. *A. barbadensis* (also known as *A. vera*) is commonly called medicine-plant or burn aloe, since it is most widely known for the healing properties of its sap. It is a stemless plant with green leaves and yellow flowers. *A. variegata* (tiger aloe) has white-spotted green leaves in triangular rosettes. Pink to dull red flower clusters appear intermittently throughout the year.

Crassula
Airplane-plant, baby jade, jade plant, moss crassula, rattail crassula, rattlesnake, scarlet-paintbrush, silver jade plant

Crassulas form a widely diversified plant group, characterized by unusual and varied leaf forms, arrangements, and colors. *C. argentea* (jade plant, baby jade) is popular and easy to grow. A compact, tree-like succulent, it has stout, branching limbs with oblong, fleshy leaves 1 to 2 inches long. In direct sunlight, the smooth, dark green leaves become tinged with red. *C. arborescens* (silver jade plant) has gray leaves with red margins and seldom flowers. *C. falcata* (scarlet-paintbrush, airplane-plant) is known for long, sickle-shaped, gray-green leaves and clusters of scarlet flowers above the foliage. *C. lycopodioides* (moss crassula, rat-tail crassula) is good for hanging baskets.

Echeveria
Echeveria, hen and chicks, pearl echeveria

All echeverias have in common a rosette form. Their leaf color ranges from pale green through deep purple. Many are luminous pink in full sun. *E. elegans* (pearl echeveria) forms a tight rosette of small, whitish green leaves. Rose flowers tipped with yellow are borne on pink stems in spring or summer. *E.* 'Morning Light' is a hybrid that has rosettes of luminous pink foliage.

Euphorbia
African-milkbarrel, corkscrew, cow's-horn, crown-of-thorns, living-baseball

The genus *Euphorbia* is too diverse to allow more than a few generalizations. All species have a toxic, milky sap. Mature sizes range from a few inches to many feet. The leaves are generally insignificant and deciduous. Many species have spines, though unlike cacti spines, they do not grow out of areoles. The flowers are usually quite small, often yellow or greenish yellow. Euphorbias require a slightly richer soil than do most succulents and they do need bright light.

Kalanchoe
Kalanchoe, Christmas kalanchoe, felt-plant, flaming-katy, pandaplant

Kalanchoes are grown for both their flowers and foliage. The leaves of *K. beharensis* (felt-plant) are large and triangular with curving, rippling edges. Their brown hairs give them a felty appearance. Pink flowers appear in spring. *K. blossfeldiana* (Christmas kalanchoe, flaming-katy) produces heads of brilliant scarlet, orange, or yellow flowers on thin stems 15 inches high. Its shiny, green, oval leaves are tinged with red. *K. tomentosa* (pandaplant) grows to 15 inches. Plump, pointed leaves that are covered with silvery hairs and tipped with rust brown bumps branch from a central stem.

Living-stones

Living-stones are perhaps the most interesting of all succulents. This group of several genera with similar cultural requirements resembles small rocks, mimicking their natural environment. They can be particular in their cultural requirements and are not recommended for beginning gardeners. They need minimal watering when not flowering and are usually best propagated from seed.

Conophytum grows in stemless, clumping leaf pairs. Its round, thick foliage ranges in color from blue-green and gray-green to yellow-green. The leaves are often speckled and usually have "windows," or small slits, at the top, which form the division between the leaves. White to yellow flowers, like dandelions, appear from the slit.

Fenestraria (window-plant, baby-toes) has thick, dull green, stemless leaves that clump to form a 2- to 2½-inch rosette. The leaves have slits at the top. The yellow or white daisy flowers are borne on a short stem above the leaves.

Lithops has short leaves that imitate both the shape and the coloring of rocks. It grows in stemless clumps of paired leaves approximately 1 to 2 inches in diameter. Yellow to white dandelionlike flowers emerge from between the leaves. Lithops needs very-fast-draining soil.

Sansevieria trifasciata
Sansevieria, snakeplant, mother-in-law's-tongue

One of the hardiest of all indoor plants is *Sansevieria*. Erect, dark green, lance-shaped leaves emerge from a central rosette. Golden yellow stripes along the margins and horizontal bands of grayish green create a striking pattern similar to the coloring of an exotic snake. *S. trifasciata* 'Laurentii' has wide, creamy yellow stripes along the leaf edges. Dwarf sansevierias include *S. trifasciata* 'Hahnii' and *S. trifasciata* 'Golden Hahnii'. A relative, *S. cylindrica*, has round leaves with pointed tips. Mature plants produce fragrant, pink or white blooms in spring.

Sedum
Donkey's-tail, burro's-tail, jellybeans

S. morganianum (donkey's-tail, burro's-tail) is a trailing, slow-growing succulent, ideal for hanging containers. Its light gray to blue-green leaves are ½ to 1 inch long, oval, and plump. The 3- to 4-foot trailing stems, densely covered with these leaves, create a braid or rope effect. The leaves will break off easily. Also, a powdery bluish dust covering the leaves is called bloom.

Senecio
Cocoon-plant, gooseberry-kleinia, string-of-beads

Senecio is a large and widely varied genus that includes small succulents, hanging or climbing vines, and large shrubs. The stems of all the succulent species are spineless, supporting leaves that are spherical and thick or flat and elongated. The small daisy flowers come in yellows, whites, and reds. Some are petalless. They are borne at the ends of the stems in summer. String-of-beads (*S. rowleyanus*) has hanging stems with unusual, ½-inch, spherical leaves that look like light green beads. Small, fragrant, white flowers appear in winter.

Care of Succulents

Light: Place in a bright, indirectly lit south, east, or west window.
Water: Water thoroughly when the soil ½ inch below the surface is dry. Discard drainage.
Humidity: Dry air is fine.
Temperatures: 50° to 55° F at night, 65° to 70° F during the day.
Fertilization: Fertilize lightly with a low-nitrogen fertilizer in spring and summer. Fertilize more lightly through fall and winter for succulents that grow actively the year around.
Propagation: Stem cuttings and offsets root easily. Dry the offset or cutting for a few days until a callus forms, then plant in well-drained potting mix and keep barely moist. Many succulents can also be reproduced from leaf cuttings.
Grooming: Cut off flower stalks as the blooms age.
Repotting: Repot only every 3 or 4 years, when essential. Use a shallow pot and a very porous soil.
Problems: Root rot can result from soggy soil caused by poor drainage or excessive watering. Stem and leaf rot may be caused by cool, damp air. Leaves wilt and discolor from too much water, especially in winter. Brown dry spots are caused by underwatering.

Sansevieria trifasciata

Sedum morganianum

Senecio rowleyanus

INDEX

Page numbers in boldface type indicate principal references; page numbers in italic type refer to illustrations or photographs.

110

U.S. Measure and Metric Measure Conversion Chart

		Formulas for Exact Measures			Rounded Measures for Quick Reference		
	Symbol	When you know:	Multiply by:	To find:			
Mass (Weight)	oz	ounces	28.35	grams	1 oz		= 30 g
	lb	pounds	0.45	kilograms	4 oz		= 115 g
	g	grams	0.035	ounces	8 oz		= 225 g
	kg	kilograms	2.2	pounds	16 oz	= 1 lb	= 450 g
					32 oz	= 2 lb	= 900 g
					36 oz	= 2¼ lb	= 1000 g (1 kg)
Volume	pt	pints	0.47	liters	1 c	= 8 oz	= 250 ml
	qt	quarts	0.95	liters	2 c (1 pt)	= 16 oz	= 500 ml
	gal	gallons	3.785	liters	4 c (1 qt)	= 32 oz	= 1 liter
	ml	milliliters	0.034	fluid ounces	4 qt (1 gal)	= 128 oz	= 3¾ liter
Length	in.	inches	2.54	centimeters	⅜ in.		= 1 cm
	ft	feet	30.48	centimeters	1 in.		= 2.5 cm
	yd	yards	0.9144	meters	2 in.		= 5 cm
	mi	miles	1.609	kilometers	2½ in.		= 6.5 cm
	km	kilometers	0.621	miles	12 in. (1 ft)		= 30 cm
	m	meters	1.094	yards	1 yd		= 90 cm
	cm	centimeters	0.39	inches	100 ft		= 30 m
					1 mi		= 1.6 km
Temperature	°F	Fahrenheit	⅝ (after subtracting 32)	Celsius	32° F		= 0° C
	°C	Celsius	⅝ (then add 32)	Fahrenheit	212° F		= 100° C
Area	in.²	square inches	6.452	square centimeters	1 in.²		= 6.5 cm²
	ft²	square feet	929.0	square centimeters	1 ft²		= 930 cm²
	yd²	square yards	8361.0	square centimeters	1 yd²		= 8360 cm²
	a.	acres	0.4047	hectares	1 a.		= 4050 m²